Jazz Gui

"Wandering around N   ble upon good jazz. B_ ..... .ue right guide, one finds secret spaces, cultural combustion, and sounds that just don't exist elsewhere. Dollar is such a guide; he has the wit, wisdom, and wiliness of a seasoned vet, and a poet's pen."

Larry Blumenfeld, *Jazziz*

"Dollar provides the assured guidance of an insider who's done the hangs and knows musicians, and his writing is accessible, while still being insightful enough to speak to even seasoned jazz fans, with a dash of New York attitude and humor. Here you'll get the low-down on such things as late-night jam sessions and out-of-the-way places that only a privileged few know about, as well as where to find big band swing in midtown. Something for both the visiting jazz fans and locals looking to expand their horizons, *Jazz Guide: New York City* delivers on the promise of its title."

CMJ New Music Report

"...a slender book that's fat on jazz knowledge and lore in the Big Apple...Besides providing an insider tour of hipster clubs, mucho-cool record shops and nocturnal hangouts located all around the isle of Manhattan, Dollar stops occasionally along the way to give a mini-history lesson....Wanna know how to snag a good seat to celebrity-gawk when Woody Allen plays his clarinet during his weekly gig with a ragtime band at the high-rent Café Carlyle? It's in the book..."

Tallahassee Democrat

"*Jazz Guide New York City* is as slick and as cool as its subject. Author Steve Dollar writes with insight, intelligence and the refreshing honesty of a club regular....an essential guide for those who want to decipher the labyrinthine Gotham clubland. You'll find gems here you never knew existed..."

Pittsburgh Tribune-Review

"Without straying far from basic listings of New York's jazz haunts, this gracefully written guide also pulls off a revealing history of the genre from big bands to Dixieland to experimental jazz...Along the way you'll learn more than you thought there was to know about Mingus, Davis, Coltrane, Parker and other big names."

San Francisco Chronicle

"Pop culture critic Steve Dollar has penned a richly anecdotal and quite wonderful guide to New York City's jazz clubs...He writes knowingly about jazz landmarks, hip record stores, and jazz chains. He paints miniature portraits of jazz greats and legendary neighborhoods and laments the passing of now-defunct clubs....In Dollar's priceless book, we learn where well-known musicians were 'discovered' and much more...this guide is a must for anyone interested in the music."

Chicago Tribune

"With a strong sense of history and a nose for detail, this outgoing book provides a neighborhood-by-neighborhood analysis of relevant venues, jam sessions, subway stops, and speakeasies. Yes, Bird lives—but where?"

Mitch Myers, contributor to *Downbeat* and National Public Radio

"Respected journalist and pop culture critic Steve Dollar has the answers in spades: his *Jazz Guide: New York City* is a comprehensive guide to all the jazz clubs in New York City...Dollar has you covered and he puts *Time Out New York* to shame...Oh, the wry wit! Dollar even travels into jazz past to offer anecdotes on Sonny Rollins' fabled tenure atop the Williamsburg Bridge and the fabled 52nd Street and Harlem jazz scenes. Some of the book's highlights are the bittersweet reviews of venues that have gone to that great 52nd Street in the sky...If you're heading to New York to check out some jazz we suggest you check out *Jazz Guide: New York City* first."

Jazz Times

JAZZ GUIDE: NYC

THE LITTLE BOOKROOM
NEW YORK

JAZZ

2nd EDITION

GUIDE

NYC

STEVE DOLLAR

Book design: Chad Roberts / Louise Fili Ltd

Library of Congress Cataloging-in-Publication Data

Dollar, Steve.
Jazz guide : New York City / by Steve Dollar. — 2nd ed.
p. cm.
ISBN-13: 978-1-892145-43-7 (alk. paper)
ISBN-10: 1-892145-43-X (alk. paper)
1. Jazz—New York (State)—New York—History and criticism.
2. Musical landmarks—New York (State)—New York—Guidebooks.
3. New York (N.Y.)—Guidebooks. I. Title.
ML3508.8.N5D65 2006
781.6509747'1—dc22
2006020977

Published by The Little Bookroom
1755 Broadway, 5th floor, New York, NY 10019
(212) 293-1643 Fax (212) 333-5374
editorial@littlebookroom.com
www.littlebookroom.com

Distributed by Random House and in the UK and Ireland by
Signature Book Services

CONTENTS

INTRODUCTION · 9

TRIBECA & SOHO · 11

WEST VILLAGE · 19

LOWER EAST SIDE & EAST VILLAGE · 41

CHELSEA · 67

MIDTOWN · 73

UPPER WEST SIDE · 99

HARLEM · 107

BROOKLYN & QUEENS · 123

BEYOND THE CLUBS · 153

INDEX · 172

INTRODUCTION

THOUGH MANY AMERICAN CITIES ARE IDENTI-
FIED WITH DIFFERENT PHASES AND PERSONAS
central to the music—whether they be Louis Armstrong's New Orleans or Count Basie's Kansas City—
jazz begins its second century as an indivisible part of
the cultural life of New York City. No place in the world
has such a concentration of jazz venues and musicians,
and though the music has generated important international scenes, its roots remain vibrant in dozens of
creaky basement lounges, noisy cafes, polished supper
clubs, tony concert halls, and weathered storefronts
across the boroughs.

Jazz Guide: New York City maps this territory,
and attends to its constant flux, noting matters of historical or mythological significance, stray bits of colorful lore, incidental details regarding ambiance and
location, and, of course, what sorts of sounds usher
forth from the bandstand. This second edition picks
up where the original 2003 guide left off, with the
growth of an active new club circuit in Brooklyn and
the arrival of the slick new Jazz at Lincoln Center on
Columbus Circle. It was enough time for one much-
loved club—Smalls, in the West Village—to close
and reopen, and for a stunning renovation of Louis
Armstrong's home in Corona Park, Queens, to finally
be completed. Shuttered for ages, Minton's Playhouse,
the Harlem club where bebop was born, came back to
life. Meanwhile, the Bowery stronghold CBGBs, which
had quietly hosted a jazz series for several years, ended
its three-decade run.

And so it goes. Jazz in New York is an ever-chang-
ing proposition that never goes out of style, not unlike
the city that has so faithfully fostered its evolution.
This guide intends to show you why.

Steve Dollar, New York City

JAZZ GALLERY • 12
ROULETTE • 14
S.O.B.'S • 15

TRIBECA & SOHO

JAZZ GALLERY

290 Hudson Street Between Dominick
& Spring Streets

☎ 212 242 1063 · www.jazzgallery.org

🚇 Spring Street C/E, Houston Street 1

GIVEN THE RANGE OF YOUNG AND UNUSUALLY GIFTED TALENT THAT GETS A JUMP-START HERE, it's easy to think of the Jazz Gallery as one of those high-end joints where attitude prevails and insider chatter percolates like Morse code. Instead, the Jazz Gallery is a casual, welcoming venue that has become a favorite of critics and musicians. They all testify to the curatorial savvy of founder Dale Fitzgerald, whose persistence on behalf of new sounds has erected an important platform for composers and their audiences.

Fitzgerald took a detour from his interests in anthropology to plunge headlong into the business end of the New York jazz world, clocking stints at fabled spots like the Village Vanguard and the Tin Palace, and a period managing the career of trumpeter Roy Hargrove. Since then, he has taken to fostering the work of successive generations of new jazz thinkers. Some of today's sharpest, like pianists Jason Moran and Vijay Iyer, got immeasurable mileage from early stints at the Jazz Gallery. So if you want to catch an echo from the future, drop by some evening. But don't expect to hear a cash register chime distractingly as the alto player hits a high note. The venue is a non-profit space—indeed, a gallery—whose upstairs space is all polished wood floors and white walls. The bar resembles a kitchen at an Episcopal after-party: a jug or two of wine and some plastic cups. All the better to focus attention on the music, and the photographic exhibits that often grace the walls. Fitzgerald, a Rhode Island native who introduces performers in the authoritative baritone of a late-night DJ, draws much from his life as a scholar of African music, and uses the venue to explore the influences of non-Western cultures on jazz. He also foregrounds the music's connections to the visual arts, and, as he puts it, "champions the cause of living and growing jazz, rather than a jazz orthodoxy based on canonical principles..." Non-profit status helps. The venue is chartered by the state of New York as a museum, and acts as a conduit for artists seeking grants and commissions for new work. Musicians get in free, which makes it a good spot for fans to strike up a conversation with well-known performers who happen by.

Beyond its ambitions, the venue also exists within a pocket of New York jazz history. Fitzgerald has collected all manner of artifacts that are housed there: the sign from the Tin Palace, an influential Bowery club that enjoyed a resounding run in the late 1970s; the door to Bradley's, the much-lamented piano bar near New York University; a piano that belonged to Carmen McRae; an array of jazz poster art. Even its location is a bit mythic. The site, formerly a rehearsal space for Hargrove's bands, sits in what once was known as the city's printing district, a formerly roughneck area not far from the west side docks that were dominated by Italian-owned businesses—at least until the mid-1960s. If you wanted to hear great jazz back then, you would have haunted the Half-Note, a club whose original location is right across the street from the Jazz Gallery. There played Wes Montgomery, Jimmy Rushing, John Coltrane, Lennie Tristano, and Anita O'Day.

Fitzgerald, happy to follow in such giant footsteps, digs up an old clip from *The New Yorker*, an entry in "Goings on About Town" from September 1959, which describes the Half-Note as a "little old Quonset hut but converted into a study hall for advanced thinkers. The present set of monitors is under the control of Zoot Sims and Al Cohn. Closed Mondays."

ROULETTE

20 Greene Street between Canal & Grand Streets

☎ 212 219 8242 · www.roulette.org

🚇 Canal Street A/C/E/N/R/6/J/M/Z/1

A HOLDOVER FROM THE DAYS WHEN SOHO AND ITS ENVIRONS BOASTED A THRIVING GALLERY and performance loft scene, Roulette is following such predecessors as The Kitchen into new digs. The non-profit organization was in transit for a few years, having abandoned the TriBeCa loft where it had presented shows since 1980 — deep in the heart of De Niro Country. It has taken over a site owned by Location One, an experimental art gallery that is, likewise, a vestige of a SoHo that existed before Pottery Barn moved in and the paparazzi swooped down to stalk Lindsay Lohan.

Overseen by composer and trombonist Jim Staley, Roulette has produced between 50 and 90 concerts a year, securing grants to commission the composers it invites to play. The range is broad, with a strong focus on new jazz and contemporary music works, improvised collaborations, and one-time special events. Under-30 composers are as likely to be heard as such major downtown figures (and board members) as John Zorn or William Parker. Over the years, it's established a small record label (Einstein) and a cable access show (Roulette TV, Fridays at 11 p.m. on the Manhattan Neighborhood Network) that features interviews and taped performances. The new space, with its high ceilings and elegant interior columns, is not as funky or personable as Staley's former makeshift concert hall (i.e., his living room), but the serene environment is ideal for focused listening.

S.O.B.'S

204 Varick Street at West Houston Street
☎ 212 243 4940 · www.sobs.com
🚇 Houston Street 1

GOING STRONG SINCE 1982, THIS IS ONE CLUB WHERE MUSIC AND DANCING ARE AS COMPATible as rum and Coca-Cola. It's not really a jazz club. The initials are no euphemism—they stand for Sounds of Brazil. But the venue's exceptional taste in all things tropical and subtropical means that fans of what Jelly Roll Morton called "the Spanish tinge" in jazz can indulge fully in various African, Caribbean, and South American sources that have all informed jazz. Dizzy Gillespie collaborated with Mario Bauzá, Pérez Prado, and Cuban percussionist Chano Pozo in the 1940s. Stan Getz got together with João Gilberto in the 1960s to coax a craze for gentle samba melodies. More contemporary performers, such as trumpeter Jerry Gonzalez and percussionist Cyro Batista, keep that fusion of polyrhythms and jazz improvisation at once crisp and seductive.

S.O.B.'s, with its colorful interior and checked tile floors, offers both intimacy—the bandstand is positioned on the long wall, and is buffeted by a table seating area in the rear and an elevated bar area in the front—and elbow room. There's never ANY parking on the dance floor, though the mambo-challenged should drop by Mondays at 7 p.m. for the weekly dance classes that precede La Tropica night. Such departed masters as Tito Puente and Eddie Palmieri were received as heroes here, and the stage has been an important outpost for Cuban artists whose entry into the United States is increasingly challenged by immigration—like the hypnotic Los Mūnequitos de Matanzas, a catch-'em-when-you-can percussive outfit whose Santeria rhythms can propel even the least balletic Anglos into hip-twitching ecstasy.

DAVID GAGE STRINGS

36 Walker Street near Church Street

☎ 212 274 1322 · www.davidgage.com

🚇 Canal Street A/C/E/N/R/1

J AZZ BASSISTS IN NEW YORK CITY HAVE BUT ONE MECCA: DAVID GAGE'S INSTRUMENT SHOP in TriBeCa. It is the beginning and the end of big stringed doghouses and fancy overgrown fiddles, at once a seeming graveyard of scarred old husks and a beauty parlor of burnished, whiskey-colored rhythm machines. The shop, which occupies three floors of an old warehouse space in a once solely industrial stretch of Walker Street, is all dusty countertops and squinty-eyed purpose; its main floor is devoted to repair work, and has been featured as a backdrop for a Hewlett-Packard ad. Movie location scouts are likewise in love with the setting, which is hard to find in the neighborhood these days.

The entrance area also doubles as a gallery. There are perhaps 100 different autographed photos of the shop's clients, and a knowledgeable fan could spend a good hour simply seeking and identifying favorites.

And even if you don't play bass, the workshops hosted here are worth checking out. They usually evolve into much more than how-to clinics. Contemporary names such as Ron Carter and Dave Holland have entertained, as has Edgar Meyer from the classical side. There is no set schedule for the show-and-tell sessions, which are presented on Mondays or Tuesdays after business hours in a roomy second floor loft space that also is the instrument showroom. Check the website for updates.

55 BAR • 20

ARTHUR'S TAVERN • 22

ARTURO'S • 23

BLUE NOTE • 25

CORNELIA STREET CAFÉ • 27

FAT CAT • 29

THE GARAGE RESTAURANT
& CAFÉ • 30

SMALLS • 31

SWEET RHYTHM • 34

VILLAGE VANGUARD • 35

ZINC • 38

WEST VILLAGE

55 BAR

55 Christopher Street at Seventh Avenue South

☎ 212 929 9883 · www.55bar.com

🚇 Christopher Street/Sheridan Square 1

CONSIDERING HOW MUCH BOOZE MOVES ACROSS ITS AMPLE BAR, WHICH RUNS THE FULL LENGTH of the basement-level space, it's surprising to consider how good and how consistent live music has been at this Greenwich Village staple—for which the term "late night hang" might as well be trademarked.

The bar takes its name from its street address— 55 Christopher Street—next door to the former site of the Stonewall Inn, a gay bar where a riot erupted in 1969 after a raid by plainclothes policemen: a watershed moment in the gay liberation movement. Social history is now a plaque. And the neighborhood is quite sedate, save for the occasional mass of drunken collegiates or panhandling street kids. Though the 55 has passed through many hands since opening in 1919—its original owner is said to have won it in a card game on a steamer coming home from World War I—it has sustained its status as a lively music spot since the early '80s. That would approximate the first time electric guitarist Mike Stern plugged in his amp at the former dive bar. Along with guitarist wife Leni Stern, he's been the artist most likely to hold audiences captive here—never missing a Monday or Wednesday when he isn't on tour. The room fills up quickly, ideal for performers with intense cult followings. The latest shift in management has seen an increased focus on jazz—from fusion and funk-tinged outfits to more left-leaning approaches—with shows every night, and cover charges in the $5-$15 range.

What you can get, on a good night, is an intimate perspective on what many of the city's better young players and bandleaders are thinking about. During a recent week or two, you could have seen bands anchored by in-demand drummers Ben Perowsky and Kenny Wollesen, up-and-coming vocalist Kendra Shank, and burning ensembles fronted by the likes of saxophonist Tim Berne or trumpeter Dave Ballou: *musicians'* musicians.

The stage (OK, the floorspace in front of the back wall before you hit the bathrooms) is only part of the story. The 55 also is a place where musicians come to socialize. An entry on Cecil Taylor, who became a Picasso of modern jazz in the 1960s, in noted contemporary music authority Richard Kostelanetz's *The Dictionary of the Avant-Gardes*, implies that the leonine pianist is a recluse. In which case, the 55 is his hermetic lair. "Cecil would be hanging out in the back by the ice machine, for hours, even in daytime, surrounded by the faithful, both wasted and sober," recalls Brian Moran, who served drinks at the 55 for 15 years. "He's got a cigarette in one hand, a Brandy Alexander in the other. And he's telling stories. Jazz, Coltrane, Dolphy, dance, Baryshnikov, Martha Graham, history lessons, anecdotes, opinions. Right before he makes a point he always pauses, takes a drag off the ever-present cig: 'And then I said to John...'"

The 55 is a great place to begin a career or to end one. Norah Jones, Grammy's baby in 2003, got discovered here. Well, in at least one version of her star-is-born creation myth. And not too long before he met his tragic demise 1987, the legendary (and frightfully self-abusive) Jaco Pastorious could be glimpsed in the bar getting dinner. "He grabbed half my sandwich and ate it," Moran says. "And then he said, 'Hi, my name is Jaco. I'm the best goddamn bass player in the world.'"

ARTHUR'S TAVERN

57 Grove Street at Seventh Avenue South

☎ 212 675 6879 · www.arthurstavernnyc.com

🚆 Christopher Street/Sheridan Square 1

SINCE THERE'S NEARLY ALWAYS LIVE MUSIC GOING HERE, AND IT'S ALWAYS FREE, AND likewise funky and boisterous, this granddaddy of West Village pubs usually draws one of the youngest crowds allowable by law. This is a nice way of saying that if you're nostalgic for beer-tossed nights on the Quad, Arthur's may be your Shangri-La. The convivial and often patron-stuffed bar has its charms: After more than 60 years in business, it's found a foolproof formula. Part of that is crowd-pleasing music that doesn't overly tax the cerebral cortex. But somehow, pianist Eri Yamamoto manages to engage the ear and still offer something to think about. The Japanese-born player and composer holds down a Thursday-Saturday residency at Arthur's, working the 6:30 to 9 p.m. slot. She's well worth catching, a performer of lyricism and acutely developed tastes who is only the latest promising jazz act to pass under the bar's traditional red awning. The nightspot also claims Charlie Parker as a onetime regular, and once hosted popular trumpeter Roy Hargrove, back when he headlined at cozy corners such as this.

ARTURO'S

106 West Houston Street at Thompson Street

☎ 212 677 3820

🚇 West 4th Street A/C/E/F/V/B/D

MORE A GREENWICH VILLAGE INSTITUTION THAN A JAZZ CLUB, THIS OLD-SCHOOL ITALIAN restaurant nonetheless boasts live music every night of the week. You squeeze by the baby grand piano en route from the bar to the ancillary dining room. Behind the tip jar sits one of the proud, the few, the irascible old guys who hold down those 88s, and have been seemingly forever. That's appropriate, since Arturo's represents a warmer, more idiosyncratic phase in the life of its neighborhood, which is bordered by New York University and SoHo. Though its owner and namesake Arturo died in early 2006, the walls forever speak his name: They're a personal museum of acquaintance and enthusiasm, crowded with frames of forgotten celebrities and would-be starlets, and a unique collection of this Sunday painter's still-lifes and portraits (Marilyn Monroe is an obvious favorite, and for $150 she can be yours).

The Brick-oven Pizza That Time Forgot is among the city's most satisfying, and the music is, likewise, unfussy, with plenty of cheese dripping off the crust. Harry Whitaker, who plays several nights a week, walked into Arturo's 12 years ago, was asked to substitute for another musician, and never left. Whitaker, now 63, was the former musical director for the pop singer Roberta Flack. He grew weary of the road, but wanted to keep his fingers flexible for the studio, where he continues to write and produce jingles and the occasional group session. "I'm the only guy in New York who has a steady gig," he jokes.

Whitaker can play with a crisp attack, and relishes classic melodies from his mental jukebox of standards and hard-bop favorites. His rhythm section is typically much younger—the sideman stint at Arturo's has been a rite-of-passage for many novice jazzers—and multiple sets are generously sprinkled through the evenings. Any of them can resemble something from *American Idol*, as patrons take their turns on the mike: perky Japanese girls, matrons in from Jersey, moonstruck date night couples. Even the random actor and Arturo's addict, like Jill Hennessy or Matt Dillon, may grab the mic. You never know. Sometimes, there's a real surprise. Sometimes, you just crave that extra cheese.

BLUE NOTE

131 West 3rd Street between Sixth Avenue
& MacDougal Street

☎ 212 475 8592 · www.bluenote.net

🚇 West 4th Street A/C/E/F/V/B/D

AMERICAN VERNACULAR MUSIC WOULD NOT EXIST WITHOUT THE BLUE NOTE, WHICH YOU can explain as something played or sung deeper and darker than routinely called for—flatted, exaggerated, bitten off, made to sting or cry. It's that alchemical element in blues and jazz (and bluegrass and rock) that expresses powerful, wordless feelings. The phrase is at once fundamental and generic, particularly in jazz parlance, where it proliferates: the Blue Note record label is the most recognized name in the fraction of the music industry devoted to jazz, and has the most illustrious back catalog; there's the Duke Ellington song "Ridin' on a Blue Note," first recorded in 1938; and there's the Blue Note. The high-end Greenwich Village jazz club belongs to a chain of venues, including B.B. King's near Times Square—a 1,000-person capacity club that occasionally hosts a star like Sonny Rollins or the stray Cuban legend—four Blue Notes in Japan, and one in Milan.

Open since 1981, the Blue Note hails from the era when venues such as the Village Gate, the Half Note, the Purple Onion, and Gerde's Folk City were still in business, echoing the vitality of the 1960s. Yet, in many ways, the Blue Note is singular, perched atop the food chain, with its brass-and-mirror décor, $15 cheeseburgers, and a booking policy that tends to lure the kind of names that patrons are willing to pay more to see in such a relatively small venue (though the dining room/stage area is happily spacious for a Village establishment, holding about 200 patrons). This is where pianists such as Chick Corea and Keith Jarrett, who typically fill concert halls, choose to play and record when they want to do a run at a nightclub. This is where pianists such as Chick Corea and Keith Jarrett, who typically fill concert halls, choose to play and record when they want to do a run at a nightclub. This is where Dizzy Gillespie spent a month celebrating his 75th birthday, and Roy Haynes marked his 80th. This is where Bill Cosby or Stevie Wonder or Kim Cattrall might happen to pop up. If it's a stiffer ticket, well, you get what you pay for, and often enough, you can only get it here. There's a striving for eventfulness to go with the plentiful souvenirs on sale: jazz greats rocking steady a decade past retirement age love to stage birthday concerts here, crowding the stage with special guests and playing way past bedtime. Sometimes, the music moves in ways for which savvy commercial programming can't account.

The club has begun taking more interest in presenting players who linger slightly out of the mainstream's frame of reference, like the powerhouse Baltimore pianist Lafayette Gilchrist—a dazzling syncopator who fuses Monkish wit with the rhythmic drive of 1970s go-go music—who enjoyed a showcase on an off-night not long after he appeared there as a sideman in tenor monster David Murray's quartet. Indeed, the Blue Note may be most notable when the marquee is least adorned with stars: The late-night groove series, a kind of after-party that follows weekend headline sets, is one of the better bargains in Jazzville, mixing up jam-rock, soul, hip-hop and DJ elements into an appealingly low-down fusion.

Not every night at the Blue Note promises a revelation or a rave. Sometimes, it's just an occasion to take your mom to swoon over a telegenic crossover act, like trumpeter Chris Botti. But every so often there's something there when you need it (and still have some headroom left on the credit card).

CORNELIA
STREET CAFÉ

29 Cornelia Street between Bleecker
& West 4th Streets

☎ 212 989 9319 · www.corneliastreetcafe.com

🚇 West 4th Street A/C/E/F/V/B/D

LIKE SO MUCH ABOUT ITS NEIGHBORHOOD, THIS RESTAURANT AND BASEMENT PERFORMANCE space pours on the charm. Doing business since 1977, it's been around just long enough to cultivate an aura: that of the funky but well-vacuumed harbor of quirky creative types, conveniently slotted at the beginning of that picturesque red-brick maze of the West Village. Which is to say, if you leave after consuming too much wine, you can still find your way back to Sixth Avenue.

However, there's no telling where you'll end up once you descend from the upstairs dining room into the performance space downstairs. Owner Robin Hirsch was running the struggling café while pursuing his dreams in the theater when he hit upon the idea of staging productions in the building's excavated basement. Next thing he knows, people like the late Sen. Eugene McCarthy are reading their poetry and crowds are lining up for Hirsch's drama productions. "It was the very first time in the history of capitalism that a theater company was brought in to save a business," he says. Three decades later, Cornelia Street continues as a heavily trafficked cultural crossroads.

On any given evening, the program might be literary (this is where Eve Ensler gave her first public reading of *The Vagina Monologues*, Oliver Sacks is a regular), bilingual (a night devoted to contemporary issues of the Ukraine), or musical. The music is mostly jazz, and mostly worth the time of anyone with an ear for the fresh, the slightly offbeat, or the mildly exotic. On a weeknight not so long ago, you could have heard the Viennese composer Franz Koglmann, a rare bird in these climes, lead a septet of strings and reeds through a cycle of new pieces that, at times, sounded like a strange chamber dream of Ellington. Critics' faves, like saxophonists Tony Malaby and Bill McHenry, are frequent headliners. All manner of Gallic, Arabic, and Brazilian acts find their way here, as well.

Claustrophobics and guests who have difficulty squeezing into economy class airline seating may find the environs too close for comfort. The 85-person capacity of the basement—a long, narrow shoebox with exposed ceiling pipes offset by a Christmas-y use of color—often feels theoretical. Arrive late for a popular artist, and you'll be playing sardine back by the tiny bar, making lots of new friends.

FAT CAT

75 Christopher Street at Seventh Avenue South
☎ 212 675 6056 · www.fatcatjazz.com
🚇 Christopher Street/Sheridan Square 1

A ROOMIER, MORE CONVENTIONAL ANNEX OF THE WEST VILLAGE LEGEND SMALLS, THIS CLUB couldn't ask for more unpretentious surroundings. Its 8000 square feet are divided between a listening area and a pool hall. Fortunately, soundproofing and amplification ensure that customers don't confuse the click of a cue ball with the beat of a snare drum—and live music is piped into the game parlor. The music room, which is split between table seating (closer to the stage) and lounge-like furnishings in the rear, has the convivial ease of an old rathskeller. Its size is about thrice that of Smalls, and allows proprietor Mitch Borden to book bigger names—Wynton Marsalis made an early appearance—and Smalls regulars who have outgrown that compact venue. More often than not, however, the roster is interchangeable. Borden's always looking out for the little guy (or, at least, the fans living on student loans): the same cover charge also gets you into Smalls (and vice versa). Jam sessions nightly at 1:30 a.m.

THE GARAGE RESTAURANT & CAFÉ

99 Seventh Avenue South at Grove Street

☎ 212 645 0600 · www.garagerest.com

🚇 Christopher Street/Sheridan Square 1

NEVER A COVER CHARGE AT THIS LONG-TIME PIT STOP, WHICH FEATURES LIVE MUSIC EVERY night—big bands on Mondays and Tuesdays, jazz brunches on the weekends—in a chatty, extremely casual setting. It's a good choice for budget-conscious listeners who can content themselves with "greatest hits" selections from the repertory. What is life, after all, without a thoughtful run through Wayne Shorter's "Footprints" or similar fare, well-rehearsed by musicians who don't mind being part of a beer-commercial backdrop? The exposed brick walls holster abstract sculptures made from smashed-up car bodies.

SMALLS

183 West 10th Street at Seventh Avenue
www.fatcatjazz.com

🚇 Christopher Street/Sheridan Square 1

FEW VENUES ARE AS BELOVED AS THIS ONE. IN FACT, SMALLS IS SO BELOVED THAT EVEN THOUGH it closed in 2003, people from all over the world kept showing up at its door, expecting one of those magic moments they had heard about: the all-night jam sessions that stretched hours past the dawn; the random appearances by jazz superstars trading fours alongside music students just cutting their teeth; the flicker of something real and spontaneous that might never come to life in a more conventional club, with their drink minimums and revolving door attitude. They kept coming, and asking, and lamenting, until, one day, the guy who had taken over the address figured it probably wasn't going to thrive as anything else. He called up its former tenant, Mitch Borden, and invited him to take charge of the space again. And, as of early 2006, Smalls was back.

This modest room represents every jazz fan's dream. It's genuinely small, a 60-seat club sandwiched into a basement where the audience sits almost on top of the musicians. It's cheap, with a usual cover charge of $10 (plus $10 drink minimum, a concession to economic necessity—and the fact that Small's 2.0 has not only a liquor license but a full bar). There are no longer those marathon jams. Instead, it's the familiar two sets a night format. However, the bookings tap into the now-established pool of promising young talents that made the venue's reputation in the 1990s.

"It's too bad you can't make a living playing at Smalls," says Joshua Redman, the New York tenor saxophonist who enjoyed one of the biggest breakout careers of that decade. "It's really the ideal jazz venue." Though he's among the most public faces in jazz, Redman could be heard at Small's as late as 2001, joining frequent sidemen Brian Blade and Sam Yahel for gigs that led to the formation of a new touring ensemble. "There were these great opportunities to go down there and jam with these guys, and not have to deal with the same kind of attention and pressure I have when I go onstage as a leader."

The indefatigable Borden, who gave up a nursing career to start Smalls, and eats, sleeps, drinks, and frets over little else but his village jazz empire (which includes a sister club, the Fat Cat), is possessed of a missionary zeal. Some nights, you'll see him playing violin for the lines of people waiting outside the club on West 10th Street. Smalls is more than a business venture. Before the Smalls revival, he had mortgaged his house and juggled credit cards to keep the place going. His is a calling, embraced with a generosity and lack of cynicism that's rare in the Big Apple and rarer yet in the club business. He's an enabler, one who helped to foster what sounds like an oxymoron: a mainstream underground. Smalls has proven a solid launching pad for strong players of the post-Wynton generation, such as pianist Jason Lindner, who leads his own big band, and bassists Omer Avital and Avishai Cohen, who have both led their own ensembles to wider recognition.

"It's not like it used to be," Avital says, taking a break on the crowded sidewalk out front during a break between sets. "It was like a little community. You would rehearse here. You would sleep here. Now, it's become more like a regular club." As he talks, the energetic bassist glimpses Borden, a snappy trilby hat on his head, bantering with a trio of young Europeans who are reluctant to purchase the $5 poker chips the club uses as drink tokens. He finally waves them in without the extra charge. Avital smiles. "But as long as Mitch is here, it's fine."

Some costly renovations have done little to spoil the vibe downstairs. The space still feels like a kind of fantasy of a timeless Manhattan jazz experience: The music feverish and immediate, the chairs a windfall from 17 separate stoop sales. The beaming visage of Louis Armstrong gazes out at the audience from a wall poster, as Avital's quintet spills forward from the most contingent of stages.

As it happens, this is one fragment of real estate that has always been a landmark in New York nightlife. One incarnation saw the address become infamous in neighborhood nightlore: Leroy's Hideaway, one of the first gay bars in New York. During the 1960s, it was known as Café Wha?, where Jimi Hendrix turned the blues psychedelic en route to the rock 'n' roll pantheon. Smalls already claims a colorful legacy, inseparable from its owner. "Smalls IS Mitch," Redman says. "Because he keeps the price reasonable, you get an audience there that you don't get at other jazz clubs. Younger. Hip—meaning they have fresher ears. People don't go there just to drink and party. There's an integrity and purity to the feeling. You go into this storefront that you wouldn't even know what it was, and then you make a descent into the subterranean depths of the New York jazz scene. It's got a mythical quality."

SWEET RHYTHM

88 Seventh Avenue South between
Bleecker & Grove Streets
☎ 212 255 3626 · www.sweetrhythmny.com
🚇 Christopher Street/Sheridan Square 1

OPEN SINCE SEPTEMBER 2002, SWEET RHYTHM IS A NEW CONCEPT WALLPAPERED OVER THE façade of an older one. The venue occupies the same address as Sweet Basil, a widely appreciated spot that had presented music since the mid-1970s, when the owners of a health-food restaurant popular with local jazzers gradually turned the place into a nightclub. Sweet Basil closed in 2001. But there is continuity. The new incarnation is run by James Browne, Basil's music director for its last eight years.

What's different? The bookings are more international in flavor. "I want the club to represent more the reality of my record collection," says Browne, who spent 17 years as a DJ at Newark jazz station WBGO. The club continues to book plenty of capital "J" jazz—featuring prized veterans such as trumpeter Lew Soloff or saxophonist Steve Wilson—in a relaxed, upscale atmosphere where players feel free to drop by and sit in.

Carrying over from the former club are the high-quality acoustics, which can account for the multiple jazz recordings titled *Live at Sweet Basil*. The room slants off the street entrance, one long wall paneled in maple, the other constructed of rustic brick. Browne put in a new lighting design, hanging dozens of Thomas Edison bulbs from the ceiling. Their exposed golden filaments make a subtle complement to the midnight blue décor. Not, jokes Browne, that anything has really changed all that much. "The building dates to 1910 when it was a pharmacy. The bar is where the soda fountain used to be. I like to say that it was originally a pharmacy and it returned to its roots."

VILLAGE VANGUARD

178 Seventh Avenue South at West 11th Street
☎ 212 255 4037 · www.villagevanguard.com
🚇 Christopher Street/Sheridan Square 1
14th Street 1/2/3

TRUE SEEKERS OF JAZZ GRAIL CLAIM THE VAN-
GUARD AS HOLIEST OF HOLIES. JOHN COLTRANE,
as close as the music gets to an official saint, recorded
some of his most important work here in the 1960s.
So did, on various occasions over the decades, Sonny
Rollins, Bill Evans, Joe Henderson, Keith Jarrett, Mel
Lewis, Brad Mehldau, Art Pepper, Dexter Gordon,
McCoy Tyner, Joe Lovano, Earl Hines, Cannonball
Adderly, Dizzy Gillespie, Paul Motian, Tom Harrell,
and…the list goes on and on, a litany of geniuses and
characters, groundbreakers and traditionalists. At last
count, 108 albums or boxed sets have the club's name
somewhere in their title or credits. That's the kind of
mojo the Vanguard has.

"It's a place where jazz feels at home," says the
tenor saxophonist Chris Potter, who recorded Album
#107—*Lift: Live at the Village Vanguard*—there in
2003. "The sound has a lot to do with it. It's kind of
funky, and has lots of weird inflections. It sounds like
you're in someone's living room. I remember the very
first night I played there. I was there with [bebop
trumpet legend and former Charlie Parker sideman]
Red Rodney. I must have been 19. I was scared to death
anyway and sitting in the front row was [James] Moody
and Dizzy [Gillespie]. I wasn't sure how I was going to
make it through, but as soon as we started playing the
energy was so positive. I fell in love."

Up and running since 1935, when a law-school
dropout named Max Gordon decided he needed a place
to hang out, it's the one existing full-time jazz venue
in the city that can claim to have shaped musical history. This, even though it wasn't really a jazz club until

the 1950s, having previously been a forum for poets and sketch comics, among other entertainers. Before she became a screwball comedy queen, Judy Holliday got a leg up there, along with Betty Comden and Adolph Green, in a troupe called the Revuers. Gordon had fancier joints to run, so this humble cellar on Seventh Avenue, shaped roughly like a pizza wedge, sat comfortably on a back burner. Gordon had the smarts to turn the Vanguard into a jazz club about the time network television began absorbing all his regular talent. Smart, because the '50s and '60s are now remembered as a prime time for jazz. "He was no expert but he knew what he was doing," says Lorraine Gordon, Max's widow, who presides over the club with a certain imperious authority, shot through with poker-faced wisecracks. "Coltrane. Miles Davis. Dizzy Gillespie. Thelonious Monk. Well, they weren't anybody at the time. They became someone in time, because they were all great and Max knew it." Lorraine Gordon, a Newark, N.J., native whose first marriage was to Blue Note records founder Alfred Lion, knew who Max Gordon was, but never really had a conversation with him until one day on Fire Island. She began talking about a pianist her husband had recorded. "I booked Thelonious without knowing it. Don't ask me the year. Long ago. He did no business whatsoever and Max bawled me out. Max died in 1989. I continue in his spirit, in his name, in his jollity, in his meanness, in his wonderfulness. I carry the torch," she says, chuckling. "That's the beginning and end of the story."

Well, not quite. The Vanguard's contemporary profile is strong. Newer talents slip in, such as pianists Uri Caine and Ethan Iverson, if Gordon is enthusiastic enough to embrace them, while regulars return again and again. Wynton Marsalis is a loyal patron, and released a seven-disc boxed set of recordings made on the bandstand. Unshakable keepers of the faith—such as the Heath Brothers, pianist Barry Harris, and the Vanguard Jazz Orchestra, which has played every Monday night for 33 years—bolster the Vanguard's reputation as one place you can hear jazz about which there is no debate: It's definitely jazz. And on rare occasions when there is a shadow of doubt, you might hear a bartender turn critic, slamming the cash register a little bit harder to express displeasure at a particularly gnarly saxophone eruption. "I just tell them never to do it during a bass solo," Gordon says, pausing to note that, hanging above the bar (in the rear corner of the room, stage right) is the euphonium owned by the late trumpeter Jabbo Smith, one of her favorites.

The Vanguard, simply, does not concede. It serves no food (the kitchen serves as both dressing room and business office). It accepts only cash. It will eject or severely tongue-lash patrons unfortunate enough to have left their cell phones on. It only accommodates 120 people per set. "I don't know what people expect when they come here," says Gordon. "It's not Radio City Music Hall. But most of them are entranced by it because it's so pure and original. I do straighten the pictures. And I just put new doors on front. The old ones I'm going to sell on eBay."

Indeed, the club is, itself, something of an artifact. The red neon sign that identifies the Vanguard, visible for blocks up and down Seventh Avenue, may not be as iconic as the Empire State Building or the billboards in Times Square, but it signifies something integral to Manhattan and its image. And like the Berlin Wall, it seems, even busted up pieces of the venue are valuable. There's a broken light fixture above the stage that will never be repaired. "The Mingus light," Gordon calls it. "He smashed his bass into it. It's just the hollowed out part of a light. We keep it. It's a shrine. Hey, he ripped off the front doors once!"

Fewer such scenes transpire these days. But while she indulges nostalgia for the days when jazz seemed as volatile as hip-hop, Gordon has no reservations about her club's—or the music's—future. And certainly none about its present. "If I hear one more person tell me jazz is dead, and walk into a jammed room at the Vanguard, I've got to ask: What are they talking about?"

ZINC

90 West Houston Street at LaGuardia Place
☎ 212 477 8337 · www.zincbar.com
🚇 Broadway-Lafayette Street A/C/E/F/V/B/D

PRETTY CLOSE TO THE ARCHETYPE OF THE "JAZZ BASEMENT," THIS DOWNSTAIRS ROOM BECKONS from a cluster of bars and restaurants along Houston Street, a block or two from New York University. The interior, with a cushy red banquette running along one wall and a bar opposite, feels as seductively candle-lit as one of those "caves" that dot the Left Bank of Paris, tight cellars where lovers and musicians convene to escape the city's bustle. That appeal translates into true romance—at least, for those who enjoy hearing performances up close and personal. Even perched on a barstool near Zinc's entrance, you're almost on top of the small staging area a few strides away. The bar features Latin-themed performances on Thursdays and African sounds on Fridays, with Saturdays and Sundays devoted to Brazilian music. Jazz fills the rest of the calendar, most notably on Mondays when guitarist Ron Affif leads the Zinc house band, which often features the highly respected drummer Jeff "Tain" Watts. At $5 admission for all shows (plus drink minimum), it's one of the best deals in town.

5C CAFÉ AND
CULTURAL CENTER • 42

DETOUR • 45

JIMMY'S NO. 43 • 48

JOE'S PUB • 50

THE KNICKERBOCKER • 51

LOUIS • 54

MO PITKIN'S HOUSE
OF SATISFACTION • 55

NUBLU • 56

RUE B • 57

THE STONE • 60

TONIC • 62

LOWER EAST SIDE & EAST VILLAGE

5C CAFÉ AND CULTURAL CENTER

68 Avenue C at East 5th Street

☎ 212 477 5993 · www.5ccc.com

🚇 Second Avenue F/V

ONCE UPON A TIME IN THE EAST VILLAGE, THE AVENUES OF A, B, C, AND D WERE ROUGH AND edgy and riddled with the drug trade. (Well, D is hanging in there). But living was cheap, and artists flocked there—decades before the era celebrated in the bohemian rhapsody of *Rent*, itself a symptom of the neighborhood's latter-day gentrification, rather than a defiant expression of paradise lost. Charlie Parker lived on Avenue B opposite Tompkins Square Park in the 1950s. Charles Mingus resided for a while in the mid-1960s on Fifth Street near Avenue A (Sophie's, one of the last great neighborhood pubs, approximates the spot). Slug's, a dive bar on Third Street near Avenue C, was the archetypal Alphabet City jazz dive of the '60s: You could drop in for a drink, some fried chicken, and hear a wholly catholic range of performers. As swinging as Horace Silver. As astral as Sun Ra. As coruscating as Albert Ayler. If you looked around, most of the musicians weren't even playing. They were just there to hang out. You might have rubbed elbows with John Coltrane or Ornette Coleman. Or, if you were the popular hard-bop trumpeter Lee Morgan ("The Sidewinder"), you would have been shot to death—onstage—by a girlfriend, in 1972. That's life.

Despite the influx of trust-fund kids and redevelopment of former squats into high-rent apartments, the East Village is still the best place to bump into workaday musicians and old school poets, happen across a live performance in one of the few remaining community gardens, or find yourself at the Charlie Parker Jazz Festival, staged annually in the park during late August. Start out early enough, and you could also discover the 5C Café (also known as 5C Cultural

Center), a modest storefront that has been presenting shows, off and on, since 1995. Native Philadelphian Bruce Morris, who began renovating the space in 1981 while staging performances all over the neighborhood, runs 5C with a partner, Trudy Silver. Its continued existence relies on its founder's capacity for enduring a succession of legal battles—the explication of which becomes dizzyingly Byzantine. The upshot, however, is that weekend sets must conclude by 9 p.m., and weeknight events by 7 p.m. Because he came up against a "judge who hates jazz," Morris could only offer unamplified performances on piano, strings, and voice for many years. His appeals were finally heard in a more sympathetic court, and the restrictions were lifted. As of summer 2006, a challenge to the music curfew was pending.

What's serendipitous is that the reconditioned baby grand Morris has on hand sounds sweeter than most do at the fancy places. And since the room has the feel of a music den, with classic jazz LP jackets prominently displayed, along with photographs and abstract paintings (by 1960s saxophonist Marion Brown), hearing a live performance there is a wonderfully vivid experience. It's a bit like church, or a private listening party, and what shows must legally lack in pyrotechnics is more than made up for by Morris's unabashed advocacy for his cause. He's one of the last of the true believers, the kind of guy who strikes a bare-chested pose on his homepage, hoisting a trumpet in one hand and a bunch of carrots in the other. (The café, by the way, serves fresh vegetable juices, as well as caffeinated drinks; alcohol is neither available nor welcome on the premises.)

"This is a true community kind of place, the way it used to be 30 years ago," says Morris, who plays DJ Tuesday-through-Thursday nights, spinning his favorite records for anyone who drops by. Most weekday afternoons around 5, there's a solo piano set featuring someone from the neighborhood, young players like Andrew Bemkey or more seasoned ones like Charles Eubanks (a longtime member of saxophonist Dewey Redman's bands). The venue has also begun to attract fresh arrivals, recent graduates of the New School and other jazz seedbeds, who are creating their own scene. "You don't get to this city and hop right over to the Village Vanguard," Morris observes, and is happy to supply a lily pad for the aspiring. In the spirit of non-profit arts organizations (which 5C is registered as), Silver teaches music classes there, as well. "Oh, man. Those were some times," he continues, clearly sorry to have seen them go, but still holding onto his patch of jazz real estate as if it were a rare postage stamp. "You think about Slug's. It was just this little neighborhood bar, but it was happening!"

DETOUR

349 East 13th Street at Second Avenue
☎ 212 533 6212 · www.jazzatdetour.com
🚇 First Avenue L

LIKE A DEFAULT MECHANISM, DETOUR IS ALWAYS THERE. AND THERE'S ALWAYS A GROUP OF ASPIRing jazz stars playing in the back, every night. Sometimes they grow up to be a drummer like Matt Wilson, or a saxophonist like Rudresh Mahanthappa—two widely admired bandleaders with new things to say on their instruments—and they often come back for a visit. Since Detour is a bar first and foremost, and admission is free, it gets a) crowded and b) loud, even on Tuesday nights. So, the fusion-minded acts have an easier time cutting through the noise, and the hornplayers have full justification to test their lung capacities. These are not necessarily bad things, especially on evenings when musicians can pull their own crowd. And if not, the colorful regulars, a seasoned cross section of downtown bohemians and genial barflies, are often as entertaining. The bar staff is first-rate.

JAZZ AND POETRY

A GATHERING OF THE TRIBES

285 East 3rd Street between Avenues C & D

☎ 212 674 3778 · www.tribes.org

🚇 Second Avenue F/V

BOWERY POETRY CLUB

308 Bowery at Bleecker Street

☎ 212 614 0505 · www.bowerypoetry.com

🚇 Second Avenue F/V Bleecker Street 6

LANGSTON HUGHES AND KENNETH PATCHEN PER-
FORMED WITH CHARLES MINGUS. ALLEN GINS-
berg's epochal "Howl" evoked "the ghostly clothes
of jazz." Contemporary writers who first came to the
fore in the 1960s, such as Amiri Baraka, Ishmael Reed,
and Jayne Cortez, often read in the context of a live
jazz performance. Though the two don't always mate
naturally, poets and jazz musicians share an affinity for
the melodic line, the resonant pause, and the rhythms
of breath.

Poet and self-annointed "heckler"—due to his
habit of verbally harassing spoken-word newbies at
readings—Steve Cannon understands this better than
most people. He oversees activity at A Gathering of
the Tribes that is both the quintessential East Village art space and the name of a journal sufficiently
well-regarded to have attracted Wynton Marsalis as a
patron. The trumpeter recorded "Live at the House of
Tribes" before a rowdy audience there in December
2002, and the loose riffing session won Marsalis some
of his best reviews in years.

Cannon is the liveliest of hosts. He holds readings, organizes workshops, presents visual art exhibits,
and stages frequent performances (there's a lush gar-
den in the rear of the classic 19th-century tenement

building that's perfect for such occasions). He's a pure character, a blind rabble-rouser whose novel *Groove, Bang and Jive Around* achieved underground buzz status with its raunchy saga of sexcapades in 1960s New Orleans.

You might catch The Heckler some evening at the Bowery Poetry Club. The brainchild of former Nuyorican Poet's Café honcho Bob Holman, the club occupies a pleasing, thoroughly renovated street-level site across the street from the site of CBGB, the legendary punk-rock club that closed in late 2006 after more than 30 years. BPC represents the next wave of Bowery amusements, which cater strongly to the overwhelming influx of NYU students living in newly constructed highrise dorms nearby. The blonde wood floors are shiny, the ceilings are high, and the staff is friendly: This is not your grandfather's skid row. In fact, if not for the occasionally explicit content of some of the poetry, the venue could pass for a yuppie fern bar. Besides seemingly constant poetry slams, book parties, and one-man shows, there is weekly zaniness from onetime Andy Warhol movie star Taylor Mead (Fridays, 7 p.m., $5), and impressive jazz bookings. Reigning downtown jazz capos such as Butch Morris, who leads big band "conductions," and Marc Ribot, a guitarist whose travels have included stints with Elvis Costello and Tom Waits, have played here. So, too, has the music historian and Latin groove connoisseur Ned Sublette, a clarinetist whose interests veer between sonic experiments and the ecstatic rhythms of Santeria. Though it's technically a "poetry club," the bar offers much nicer surroundings than most downtown music venues. Maybe it's a sign of the times. Those "ghostly clothes" are overdue for a trip to the dry cleaners.

JIMMY'S NO. 43

43 East 7th Street between Second & Third Avenues

☎ 212 982 3006 · www.freestylejazz.com

🚇 Second Avenue F/V 8th Street N/R/W Astor Place 6

DURING THE EARLY 1980s, DEE POP WAS THE DRUMMER FOR THE BUSH TETRAS, A JANGLY, minimalist band that scrambled up punk and funk and headlined at all the celebrated dives (the Mudd Club, CBGBs) and hot spots (Danceteria) of the era. "I came out of that scene associated with punk, but I also came from an artier side that was just as much influenced by James Brown and avant-garde jazz than, say, by the New York Dolls," says Pop, whose name is an abbreviation of his Greek surname, Papadopolous. After all, he notes, the early '80s was a time when free-jazz and post-punk musicians often shared the same bandstand.

Pop keeps the faith with his ongoing Free Style Jazz Medicine Show series, which was long hosted at the now-shuttered punk shrine CBGB, and relocated in 2005 to better upholstered quarters at Jimmy's No. 43, a basement bar and restaurant that specializes in alcoholic beverages brewed by Belgian monks. The spot sits along a popular row of similar drinking establishments (including the fabled McSorley's) on East 7th Street, where ale-soaked acolytes come to indulge. On Sunday evenings, they are joined by jazz fans who are, likewise, connoisseurs. Pop has become one of the city's most astute bookers, mostly by sticking to players he knows and likes. Each week, a small working combo (typically a quartet) takes the small stage in a curious, sequestered back room, where a mounted deer head gazes from the wall and a giant chalkboard serves as a backdrop. (It may be scrawled with the abstract efforts of someone's kid who wandered back earlier in the day, a Cy Twombly in the making).

The names may be well-known (like the guitarist

John Abercrombie) or fast-rising (the jaw-droppingly dynamic drummer Tyshawn Sorey). Either way, the music is consistent, strong and forward-looking—even if the space feels, in some uncanny way, like a holdover from a 1960s Cassavettes film. There's romance in that, and the ready goblets of draught Duvel only enhance it.

JOE'S PUB

425 Lafayette Street between Astor Place
and East 4th Street
☎ 212-539-8778 · www.publictheater.org
🚇 8th Street N/R/W Astor Place 6

ONE OF THE NICEST ROOMS IN THE CITY, THIS LOUNGE AND PERFORMANCE SPACE IS FAR spiffier than the workaday term "pub" connotes. Plush lounge seating, TV studio lighting, and belfry-high ceilings give the two-tiered venue an air of luxury that makes any visit a pleasure—and explains why cocktails are $10 a pop. Named in honor of the late New York Public Theater powerhouse Joe Papp, the Pub formerly served as the non-profit's library, until it was smartly converted into a moneymaking venture with strong appeal to the music industry. Jazz is a regular attraction on a calendar that's otherwise strong on singer-songwriters, major label "tastemaker" showcases, and local artists hip enough for the room. Seating is limited to roughly 100, so most shows sell out quickly (if tickets are even available, as record companies often throw invitation-only events), and standing room only is a routine option. There's not much argument, however: You won't find a more enjoyable place to hear—and see—live music than this.

THE KNICKERBOCKER

33 University Place at East 9th Street

☎ 212 228 8490 · www.knickerbockerbarandgrill.com

🚇 8th Street N/R/W Astor Place 6

THE CLASSIC, CENTURY-OLD STEAKHOUSE NEAR WASHINGTON SQUARE OFFERS A VINTAGE, SUIT-and-tie ambiance in the shadow of New York University's ever-expanding youthplosion. Black leather booths, Hirschfeld sketches framed on the burgundy walls, marble and oak appointments—what's not to love? Besides being the spot sophomore lit scholars are most likely to drag Mom and Dad to on parent's week-end—it's close by, and they take plastic—the Knick has long been a cozy jazz den as well. Live music is featured Thursday through Sunday nights, for a mod-est $5 cover. The bookings tend toward piano-and-bass duos, with such top shelf names as Cecil McBee, Joanne Brackeen, Junior Mance, and Valerie Capers.

JAZZ HIPSTER HEAVEN

DOWNTOWN MUSIC GALLERY

342 Bowery between East 2nd & East 3rd Streets

☎ 212-473-0043/800-622-1387

www.dtmgallery.com

🚇 Second Avenue F/V Bleecker Street 6

S INGULAR IN ITS FOCUS, THE DOWNTOWN MUSIC GALLERY IS THE KIND OF RECORD STORE THAT could only exist in a novel by Nick Hornby or—the East Village. The typical customers, says owner Bruce Gallanter, "are people with hairy faces." It's the ultimate record collector mecca for those who itch for peculiar niches: the rare 10-CD box-set of futuristic Japanese electro-acoustic improv, the reissued 200-gram vinyl pressing of a long out-of-print record by electric guitar legend Sonny Sharrock, or the latest disc on one of the many artist-owned labels that dominate the lower Manhattan jazz demimonde.

The store, on a transitional block of The Bowery, belongs to a fondly remembered era before franchises and the Internet revolutionized the music retail business. One reason DMG stays afloat, though, is through its substantial mail-order traffic, and by cornering the market on avant-gardish music—whether jazz, classical, or rock—that can be difficult to find. Gallanter, a tireless advocate for new sounds, publishes a weekly newsletter (also available on the store's website) in which he reviews virtually every fresh release that comes in. He keeps an obsessively completist stock of CDs by downtown cult heroes John Zorn and Bill Laswell, and also maintains a satisfying assortment of used jazz vinyl and classic jazz titles—with a tempting discount CD display which, often as not, will boast a coveted old Wayne Shorter or Don Cherry title.

Artists often sell their product direct to the store, or drop by to check on business, so it's not unlikely for customers to bump into the very performer whose CD they're buying. To make things even easier, Gallanter hosts free concerts every Sunday at 7 p.m. The talent often is representative of a new generation of burning performers—such as saxophonist Matana Roberts—and on special occasions, a presiding master or two, like multi-reedist Oliver Lake. It's not uncommon for the crowd to spill out the door.

LOUIS

649 East 9th Street at Avenue C

☎ 212 673 1190

🚇 First Avenue L

PART OF THIS NEIGHBORHOOD'S BUDDING BAR-TOPIA, LOUIS IS A CLASSIC SHOEBOX DRESSED UP in soft hues and exposed brick. And, as it's named in honor of Louis Armstrong, it's got more going on than its wine selection. Live jazz five nights a week with a focus on piano (the bar has two uprights), and John Coltrane on the stereo for later. Record collectors will covet the display of vintage jazz 7-inch singles framed on the walls.

MO PITKIN'S HOUSE OF SATISFACTION

34 Avenue A at East 2nd Street

☎ 212-777-5660 · www.mopitkins.com

🚇 Second Avenue F/V

NAMED AFTER THE ECCENTRIC COUSIN OF OWN-ERS JESSE AND PHIL HARTMAN, THIS NEW-fangled bar and restaurant salutes the spirit of East Village bohemia while seriously upgrading the neighborhood ambience. The Hartmans are the family behind the Two Boots pizza and media empire that introduced the world to the "Mr. Pink," a slice named after onetime Avenue A habitué Steve Buscemi's character in the cult flick *Reservoir Dogs* (which is just the sort of thing that might get screened at the nearby Pioneer Cinema, another Two Boots franchise). Mo's upstairs performance space offers music, literary, and avant-cabaret bookings that are as zesty as that pizza, essentially staging a continuous version of the annual Howl! Festival that the Hartmans also put on each August. Jazz is peripheral to this: "Miles Mondays," a DJ'ed affair, is the sole staple on the calendar. The listening room is so comfortably designed, with long rows of tables perpendicular to the stage, that it's worth scoping out for the occasional visit by, say, saxophonist Roy Nathanson, or former Captain Beefheart guitarist Gary Lucas.

NUBLU

62 Avenue C between East 3rd & East 4th Streets
☎ 212-979-9925 · www.nublu.net/index.html
🚇 Second Avenue F/V

EASY TO MISS, UNLESS YOU KNOW WHAT TO LOOK FOR: A SINGLE LIGHT BLUE BULB SHINING OVER a door. Late evenings, when this informal wine bar revs up, the block it occupies is quiet, almost desolate. Next to the door, a sheet of paper is taped to the wall, with the day's date and a list of musicians. This is Nublu.

Pass through a second door inscribed with a hand-written transcript of the Haile Selassie speech that became the Bob Marley song "War," and you're in. There's no cover charge, and the setting is typical of downtown DJ hangouts: a pair of turntables in a back corner, lots of '60s retro furnishings, Edith Piaf and Miles Davis album covers as wall art, a sassy barkeep with a sultry French accent, everyone scruffy-chic and international. At the very back of the room, in what amounts to a second lounge area, a young guitar-based quartet is working through a set of rhythmic near-fusion—kind of David Sanborn gone Williamsburg.

Launched by New York saxophonist Ilhan Ersahin, the club represents an increasingly popular interface between groove-oriented and electronic music and a growing community of jazz musicians and fans in their 20s and early 30s who like to mix beats with their blue notes. Ersahin draws on his connections to various pools of players to create some promising hybrids. (You can hear them on a series of CDs promoted on the club's website). Mingus Big Band saxophonist Seamus Blake is a regular for the midnight show, for instance, with his funk outfit Bloomdaddies, as is trumpeter Eddie Henderson.

RUE B

188 Avenue B between East 11th & East 12th Streets
☎ 212-358-1700
🚇 First Avenue L

ONLY A FEW YEARS AGO, THIS SORT OF BISTRO-WITH-MUSIC WOULD HAVE STUCK OUT LIKE a sore thumb—or a Gold Card—along Avenue B. Too spiffy. Now it's the status quo. The sister restaurant to Radio Perfecto next door, Rue B has swank to burn. An upright Steinway sits in a nook near the restroom, and when musicians play here—as they do every night—patrons have to squeeze by them. If they're sitting close enough, perched on a bar stool, they could join in a duet. Owner Peter DuPre, a onetime actor and entrepreneurial concept guy, collected seating and fixtures from the Stanhope Hotel when the 1930s building was renovated. The walls are lined with deco-patterned cork or Rat Pack memorabilia. The zinc tabletops and bartop convey that industro-diner vibe. The rare XXL movie poster from photographer Bruce Weber's documentary *Broken Noses* (DuPre was a former Weber model) suggests the connoisseur's hand. When a bar is this nice, the music always sucks. Thankfully, Rue B is an exception. Performers tend to lean towards the singer-songwriter/session dude side of the jazz spectrum. Steely Dan's subversive brainiac, Donald Fagen, has been known to jam when he needs to warm up for a tour (he's a friend of the owners). Other nights, you might hear the pianist Joel Forrester (Microscopic Sextet), a local favorite who plays every Monday.

SUBWAY SOUNDS

"**I**T'S TOUGH WHEN THE CRITIC HAS A GUN," SAYS TOM BRUNO. NO, THE STOCKY DRUMMER IS NOT engaged in an escalating duel with a scribe gone ballistic. He's joking, sort of, about a key part of his audience. As often as he can, Bruno sets up his kit somewhere deep in the New York City subway system, joined by musical compatriots who make at least a chunk of their living playing for spare change. The cops who patrol these stations have come to know the clamor of Bruno's sticks as intimately as the rumble of the 4 train as it rolls into Astor Place—one of Bruno's favorite spots.

Not to worry. Bruno and his colleagues have been sanctioned by the city. New York's Finest are there to protect them. Unlike, say, the rag-tag doowoppers or amateur breakdancing crews that work the subway cars and station platforms for small coin, these players are part of Music Under New York. The program includes 100-plus acts across a range of musical styles, of which jazz is prominent. Daily performances are scattered across 25 different sites in the system. Bruno, who also performs in clubs, loves a gale-force sound shaped by a natural habitat of squealing brakes and deep subterranean echoes. These musicians play fiercely enough to scare off the subway-dwelling alligators of urban legend, but have won plenty of converts over the years. "When people say they like you, on the subway, that means they really like you," says Sabir Mateen, a tenor saxophonist ubiquitous on the downtown scene, who also gigs with rock bands such as Yo La Tengo. "You can develop a rapport with people down there."

Jazz musicians seem always to have taken to Manhattan's streets. Income varies, a daily take of $30-$40 up to $100 per person used to be common, but has been in greater flux in recent years. For a young, enterprising player, it can provide enough to scrape by while offering a chance to polish technique in a relaxed public forum. Some older artists prefer the pavement to the stage, while others view the subway gig as a useful, but temporary, stop on the way to bigger things. The most famous public musician in New York was Moondog. Blinded at 16 while playing with a dynamite cap, the native Kansan taught himself to play drums and compose, and moved to New York in 1943. Four years later, he rechristened himself Moondog, and took a spot at the corner of 54th Street and Sixth Avenue, where he held forth for the next 30 years playing a mystery music he called "Snake Time." He made his own instrument—stringed and percussive inventions with names like "oo," 'uni," and "samisen"—made records, and achieved a cult following. He favored a Viking helmet and a robe, accessorized by a spear, and wore the long white beard of a Biblical saint—or the old man of the mountain.

Such personal extravagance is rare among rank-and-file subway and street-corner stalwarts. But it does illustrate the freedom such informal stages offer. And, for musicians intrepid enough to hold their ground, it's an acid test of stamina and ingenuity. "Pharoah Sanders told me that he used to try and imitate the train," says Mateen, referring to the saxophonist who rose to attention alongside John Coltrane in the late 1960s, and subsequently became one of jazz's great, latter-day mystics. "I like to think that each sound in the subway is related to a note."

THE STONE

East 2nd Street at Avenue C
www.thestonenyc.com
🚇 Second Avenue F/V

TEMPTING AS IT IS TO READ SOMETHING ALLEGOR-
ICAL IN THE NAME OF THIS BRACINGLY MODEST
venue, opened at the burned-out former site of a Chi-
nese restaurant by composer John Zorn in 2005, it's
unwise to try too hard. The not-for-profit space, where
shows are priced religiously in the $8-$10-$15 range
and all the cash goes directly to the artists, is a blow
against various empires: the big-money world of upscale jazz, the compromised scenarios of venues that
have to sell food and drink to support the music, while
actively detracting from the quality of the listening
experience, the often draconian "percentage" system
where headliners can wind up losing money on a gig
because the club takes half the door or bills the musician for the sound engineer. And so on. Is this a David
and Goliath tale?

If you want it to be. Or else it's the latest episode
in artistic self-determination to come out of the downtown scene. Zorn named the spot after the late Irving
Stone, a tireless benefactor of jazz musicians and a
regular sight throughout the 1990s at venues such as
Tonic and the Knitting Factory, where he was joined
by his wife Stephanie (who now comes by The Stone,
and may even play piano sometimes).

The simple space is done in black and white, with
red curtains over brick and a gray floor. There's room
for about 60 folding chairs, a baby grand piano, a small
"bandstand," and a bathroom tucked into the rear corner. A different musician curates each month's schedule, which may involve a theme (solos or duos; guitars),
a tribute (to the peripatetic trumpeter Don Cherry, for
instance), or provide an occasion for a performer to
play creative mix-and-match with fellow musicians

they admire. Curators have been invited from all kinds of pockets, ranging from the violinist Carla Kihlstedt (Tin Hat Trio) to the producer Bill Laswell to the bassist William Parker. The only abiding connection is that they've crossed paths with Zorn, which isn't hard because he's been a significant presence on the scene since the late 1970s.

"Other places treat music as background," says Okkyung Lee, a cellist who often performs at The Stone and has curated a series there. "That's the feeling I get. Here, people aren't talking, they're not drinking beer, there's no noise from a bar. I don't get distracted when I play. I can really focus. I can sense that the audience is focused, too."

That's the quality that defines an evening at The Stone, which covers its expenses through sales of limited-edition CDs recorded there and through public donations. The stillness is especially welcome as performances use little or no amplification (except when necessary, as with turntables or electric guitar). As many occasions feature stringed instruments and heady improvisations, the meditative quiet is essential, and can foster a nearly Zen-like degree of concentration. Of course, the East Village being one of the rowdier neighborhoods in the city, and with the major thoroughfare of Houston Street visible from the door, there are sonic intrusions. Yet, in the democratic spirit of the music, even these have a role to play. One evening, the pianist Sylvie Courvoisier and the drummer Matt Wilson played a succinct duet in which disparate strikes of the keys (and finger-traces across the piano strings, Henry Cowell-style) were interspersed with the bleats of car horns along 2nd Street. This taught the value of silence as a sound itself. Wilson's squint at the presumptive end of the duet held the attentive audience silent on the cusp of applause. Honk! Then Courvoisier began a final trill.

TONIC

107 Norfolk Street between Delancey
& Rivington Streets

☎ 212 358 7501 · www.tonicnyc.com

🚇 Delancey Street J/M/Z/F

I F PARIS, AS WALTER BENJAMIN ONCE WROTE, WAS THE ENGINE ROOM OF THE 20TH CENTURY, then Tonic, a barebones venue in the heart of the Lower East Side, can lay claim to a similar metaphor. It's very much a salon for all kinds of 21st-century music, in permutations that include jazz—and ways that jazz is heard through such prisms as free improvisation, electro-acoustic music (can a MacBook sing the blues?), DJ culture, klezmer, Asian and European exponents and good, old-fashioned noise.

Insiders know Tonic as the club that stole the downtown jazz spotlight from the Knitting Factory when it opened in the spring of 1998. That's when club co-founders Melissa Caruso-Scott and John Scott happened on the Tonic site. The 1930s structure had once been headquarters for Kedem, a kosher winemaker, and was being run as a beauty salon (by another couple named Melissa and John, oddly enough). The club opened with a bang: a 40-night series curated by composer and avant-garde ringleader John Zorn, who had recently broken with the Knit, a club that he had been strongly identified with since 1987. Tonic was rudimentary: bare concrete floors and no air conditioning. Yet, lines spilled out the door and halfway to Delancey Street, and for many musicians it became a favored venue: Groove merchants Medeski, Martin and Wood; Zorn's various Masada ensembles; trumpeter Dave Douglas, among many others, including European free-jazz figures who occasionally tour stateside, such as saxophonist Peter Brotzmann and the late guitar pioneer Derek Bailey. The club's initial policy of inviting artists to curate month-long programs around a theme generated fascinating occasions. The venue has long since tightened-up its booking policies, advocating as much unusual rock music as jazz, and nearly went out of business in 2005 when mounting expenses prompted a series of benefit concerts and famous fans like Yoko Ono came to the club's rescue. Tellingly, so did scores of not-so-famous fans, whose testimonials are reprinted on the club's website.

Tonic's bent for musical arcana reinforces a certain defiant geekiness among the faithful. "It's like being at home," says Douglas, "and feels like you're playing for family. It's off the beaten path, which is both a big asset and a small drawback. Tonic hasn't tried to become the Disneyland of creative music. But some people who play there aren't going to draw as big an audience as they would in a more central location."

Nearly a decade on, Tonic is probably more central than it used to be: the surrounding tenements, which have housed generations of Jewish and, then, Hispanic immigrants, have been steadily converted into renovated coops, while new bars and restaurants arrive daily, their stylish young patrons spilling out onto the sidewalks to smoke and laugh. Now fully climate-controlled and a little more spruced up, the club strives to keep pace. It has expanded to accommodate about 250 people. Still, it's nothing fancy. The red curtains that run floor to ceiling behind the stage are the sole concession to décor. The young staff ("Hey, kids, let's put on a show!") and cultish devotion of the regulars, make it easy to think of Tonic as a clubhouse, albeit one without secret handshakes or initiation rituals. The basement space, which is run as a lounge called Subtonic, is more unique. Old kosher wine kegs, which stand tall and wide enough to serve as studio apartments, have been converted into private seating areas that have the feel of small wooden cabins. Business is focused on late-night DJ programs, with an emphasis on electronic soundscapes. It's also a good spot to chat with performers before or after a show. That's when the space becomes a crossroads between sonic futurism, jazz tradition, and a cyber-savvy international art culture straight out of a William Gibson novel.

ORNETTE COLEMAN OPENS AT THE FIVE SPOT CAFÉ

THOMAS PYNCHON DUBBED HIM "MCCLINTIC SPHERE" FOR HIS CAMEO IN THE 1962 NOVEL *V.*, a jazz outsider making new noises at a joint called the V-Note, where the story's vagabond Whole Sick Crew hangs out. Just three years earlier, the real-life Ornette Coleman, an unknown Forth Worth, Texas native who had arrived via Los Angeles, turned jazz audiences upside down with his debut at the Five Spot on November 18, 1959. Surely Pynchon was in attendance. So was Leonard Bernstein. So was everybody who was anybody in that neighborhood, in those days. The club, which then was situated at 4 Cooper Square, became the site for something akin to the riotous debut of Stravinsky's "Rite of Spring." Critics and fellow musicians freaked. Coleman's quartet, with Charlie Haden on bass, Billy Higgins (or sometimes Ed Blackwell) on drums, and Don Cherry on pocket trumpet, took flak for appearing to play "toy" instruments (Coleman's alto saxophone was made of plastic, Cherry's brass was, by definition, child-sized). And worse. Coleman's use of an untempered scale, and his habit of improvising on the melodic line, rather than the harmony, suggested to many ears that he simply couldn't play. In fact, he was filtering simple folk and blues themes up through Charlie Parker and laying them out in free time, and in the process changing the way in which jazz could be thought about. As Coleman's literary counterpart Sphere (also the middle name of Thelonious Monk, another Five Spot stalwart) muses, he was juxtaposing: "crazy and cool in the same molecule." Many disagreed. As Roy Eldridge told Esquire in 1961, "I listened to him all kinds of ways. I listened to him high and I listened to him sober, I even played with him. I think he's jiving, baby." But Charles Mingus offered a more enduring assessment. Coleman was "playing wrong right."

THE CUTTING ROOM • 68

THE KITCHEN • 70

CHELSEA

THE CUTTING ROOM

19 West 24th Street between
Sixth Avenue & Broadway
☎ 212 691 1900 · www.thecuttingroomnyc.com
🚇 23rd Street F/V/N/R/W

KNOWN FOR ITS PLUS-SIZE POURS OF WINE, GENTLEMAN'S CLUBROOM DÉCOR, AND ROCK-star guest lists, this favored stop for entertainment industry insiders also boasts a music room that's one of the city's better-kept secrets. Especially for jazz fans seeking a change of scenery. While bookings might include anything from a 17-piece all-female accordion orchestra (garbed in Santa Claus caps, no less) to show-case parties for pop singer-songwriters such as Sheryl Crow or Rickie Lee Jones, the venue also hosts a few jazz acts each month. Something like the New York Fusion Ensemble, a 14-piece big band that plays brassy arrangements from the Led Zeppelin songbook, often constitutes the norm; yet, the club might as easily veer towards an evening of heady avant-garde combos. There's no dominant agenda. That appears to please the many musicians who like to drop in to play, onstage or off. The Cutting Room is a favorite with house-band stalwarts from the ranks of *Saturday Night Live*, *Late Night with Conan O'Brien* and *The Late Show with David Letterman*. The connection makes sense, as co-owner Steve Walter studied composition at the Berklee School of Music in Boston with jazz vibraphonist Gary Burton. Also, his business partner is the popular New York actor Chris Noth ("Big" from HBO's *Sex in the City*, and a longtime cast member of NBC's *Law and Order*). Seems Noth wanted a place of his own to hang out and hear the music he liked, in a setting that suited his taste, and where his friends would feel comfort-able. Hence, the Cutting Room, which opened in 1999 in a cavernous warehouse space that had once housed materials for movie sets.

JAZZ RECORD CENTER

236 West 26th Street, Room 804,
between Seventh & Eighth Avenues
☎ 212 675 4480 · www.jazzrecordcenter.com
🚇 23rd Street C/E/F/V/1

HOW MANY ANGELS CAN DANCE ON THE HEAD
OF A PIN? AS ONTOLOGICAL PUZZLES GO, THAT'S
the standard issue. But here's one that's just as difficult: How many LPs are stacked, floor to ceiling, in the
Jazz Record Center?

"I can't answer that question," says Fred Cohen.
Since he's the only person in the world who conceiv-
ably could, the query deserves to be supersized to the
status of enigma. It's part of the allure of the store,
one that Cohen, who buys and sells all those records,
has been cultivating for 20 years. "I really have no
idea," he insists. "This whole thing is a hobby that got
out of hand. I haven't been miserable one day for it."

Cohen presides over a Borgesian library of vinyl
arcana, the likes of which exists nowhere outside of
public radio—probably. It's all jazz, from every era,
with some soul and gospel and blues thrown in for
variety, plus CDs, DVDs, old magazines, posters, post-
cards, and other artifacts. Though he's stumped by
the volume of albums filling the loft-like, upstairs
space, he knows what everything is worth. An obscure
Tommy Flanagan disc briefly released by a Swedish
label in the mid-1950s fetched a whopping $2,000, for
instance. But most collectibles are priced between $8
and $15. The most sought-after title? Miles Davis's
1959 masterpiece *Kind of Blue*—which is also the
best-selling jazz title in history. "It sells for upwards
of $150, even for as much as $350," notes Cohen, who
will give any record a test spin on one of two '50s-era
Thorens turntables he keeps running behind the coun-
ter. "It's one of the great prizes in any collection."

THE KITCHEN

512 West 19th Street between
Tenth & Eleventh Avenues
☎ 212 255 5793 · www.thekitchen.org
🚇 14th Street A/C/E 23rd Street C/E

THIS EMINENT ARTS SPACE IS DEVOTED TO PER-
FORMANCES OF DANCE, NEW MUSIC, MIXED
media, and theatrical works, with an emphasis on
premieres, unveilings, retrospectives, and unique collaborations. Jazz is a vital aspect of this, even as a tan-
gent. A 2003 celebration of the contemporary classical
pianist Frederic Rzewski, for instance, welcomed
disparate jazzers Arturo O'Farrill and Matthew
Shipp as opening acts. And an ongoing program of
commissions finds all manner of New York player-
composers—from jazz, improv, and new music
scenes—getting the showcase treatment. These
shows open a fascinating window on the creative
process, while also offering fresh perspectives on
the work of musicians who may not often be presented in such a fashion. The venue, pretty much
your industrial black box with bleachers and fancy
lighting design, is smack in the middle of the meat-
packing district, and not far from the galleries
of West Chelsea, so there's plenty of civic history and
trend-spotting to attend to before or after the concert.

BIRDLAND • 74

CAFÉ ST. BART'S • 76

CHEZ SUZETTE • 77

ENZO'S JAZZ AT THE JOLLY
HOTEL MADISON TOWERS • 80

IRIDIUM • 81

JAZZ AT LINCOLN CENTER • 82

JAZZ STANDARD • 88

JAZZ AT ST. PETER'S
CHURCH • 91

THE KITANO • 92

SWING 46 • 93

ZANKEL HALL • 94

BIRDLAND

315 West 44th Street at Eighth Avenue

☎ 212 581 3080 · www.birdlandjazz.com

🚇 42nd Street A/C/E

NOT TO BE MISTAKEN FOR THE ORIGINAL BIRD-LAND, WHICH WAS NAMED FOR ALTO SAXO-phonist Charlie "Yardbird" Parker and thrived on 52nd Street between 1949 and 1965, this Birdland is the latter-day version of what a stylish jazz club looks like. Tucked midway between Eighth and Ninth avenues on 44th Street, the address is just far enough away from the theater-district tourist crush to benefit from the foot traffic without being trapped by it. Though originally revived in 1986, in a smaller space on 106th Street, the franchise has been anchored here since 1995. The brassy décor, full restaurant, and dressy crowds mark it as a premium venue, as do its high-quality bookings, and the expansive sweep of its main seating area, a dining room that faces the stage (access to the bar at stage left is cheaper, but there's less of a view). If the club was a suit it would be double-breasted. If it was a car, it would be a BMW (most jazz clubs are strictly Hyundai). Though, it's all relative. Compared to the cost of a Broadway theater ticket, drinks, dinner, and a show at Birdland looks like a bargain.

Birdland makes its reputation on its commitment to big bands and orchestral jazz, and the frequency with which its showcases first-rank players. Traditionally, Monday nights in Manhattan are the province of big bands—in part, because it's a slow night, and club owners figure it's something different; in part, because big bands always seem to play on Monday nights. Birdland counter-programs, presenting vocalists on Mondays, which once were occupied by Toshiko Akiyoshi's orchestra (the pianist retired that band in 2003 but often returns with her trio). Large ensembles appear many other nights. Chico O'Farrill's Afro-Cuban Jazz Big Band nails down Sundays, as it has for years, with the late trumpeter's arrangements and an all-star cast, led by his son, pianist Arturo O'Farrill. Tuesday is for Ellingtonia, with arranger David Berger and his 16-piece Sultans of Swing. Other outfits find their way into the mix, as well as one-offs and extended runs by bandleader-composers such as Maria Schnieder, Andrew Hill, Lee Konitz, and Dave Holland. Were Gil Evans, the orchestrator of such Miles Davis epics as *Sketches of Spain* and *Porgy and Bess*, alive and kicking, he'd probably have a weekly stint, too.

CAFÉ ST. BART'S

Park Avenue at East 50th Street

☎ 212 888 2664

🚇 Lexington Avenue/53rd Street E/V

🚇 51st Street 6

THIS UPSCALE RESTAURANT HOSTS ONE OF THE MORE UNUSUAL JAZZ EVENTS IN THE CITY. LES Lieber's "Jazz at Noon" is a free weekly affair, staged Fridays at noon from mid-October through June. Lieber, who plays alto saxophone and penny whistle, and a dozen other enthusiasts from the corporate world bring their instruments, loosen their neckties, and jump into a relaxed jam session. Plenty of regulars drop by to swing a little, and remarkably so: The session's been going on for 41 years. But professional jazzers join in as well, as does each week's special guest. And the guests are no slouches. Their number has included alto saxophonist Ted Nash, guitarist Bucky Pizzarelli, reedsman Paquito D'Rivera, and trumpeter Claudio Roditi.

The setting is visibly historic: Nearby St. Bartholomew's Church, from whence the café takes its name, is a mightily impressive Episcopal sanctuary that opened in 1918. Its stunning dome arrived in 1930, based on architect Bertram Grosvenor Goodhue's design for the dome of the California State Building at the 1911 San Diego Exposition.

CHEZ SUZETTE

675B Ninth Avenue between West 46th
& West 47th Streets
☎ 212 974 9002
🚇 42nd Street A/C/E

THE MUCH-ADMIRED FRENCH BISTRO HAS ONE OF THE BETTER REPUTATIONS AMONG OLD-LINE theater district restaurants (it's been in business since 1967), and a cozy, quaint niche in Hell's Kitchen—which is scarcely hellish at all, anymore. Besides paté and osso buco, the establishment also presents a different jazz vocalist every night. The entertainment is free, and spans a range from the Francophilic to standards to the slightly further out.

LES PAUL

NOT MUCH IS CONSTANT IN NEW YORK'S JAZZ FIRMAMENT. FAVORED CLUBS COME AND GO. Great working bands get together, but can quickly disassemble as personalities or career motives dictate. The rule of thumb is: Enjoy it now, because tomorrow there will be something entirely different. The music stays fresh that way, but in jazz there's always a creative tension between tradition and innovation.

Then again, there's Les Paul. The guitarist reconciles the two seamlessly: He's the tradition of innovation. Right down to the nuts and bolts. Among many other items, Paul invented his solid-body electric guitar in 1941, using a 4x4 piece of pine with "wings" attached to it. It was dubbed "The Log," and could be amplified as loudly as necessary. (Unlike hollow body acoustic guitars, the instrument required a plug to be heard.) Thus, rock 'n' roll was made possible.

Paul relates his versions of this, and other bits of autobiography, every week at Iridium. Even though his official newsletter refers to him as "The Legend," Paul is an earthy soul who exists to blow raspberries at such notions. He's been playing somewhere in Manhattan every Monday night since 1984, though his first paying gig in the city was nearly 50 years earlier. The stint has become a ritual, beloved of tourists, ardent students of the guitar, and listeners who enjoy fleet, fancy picking complemented by the headliner's salty banter and quirky anecdotes. They line up outside the theater district site of Paul's current residency a full 30 minutes before showtime, in a queue that bends around the corner of Broadway and 51st Street. Some of the Paulites carry their own guitars (usually one of the Gibsons bearing the musician and designer's name), or an old LP. After the show, the same people will line up again for autographs. If an instrument or program isn't handy, Paul will genially take a Sharpie to an obeisant forehead.

Lester Polfus of Waukesha, Wisc., is 91 now. He wears a hearing aid, and spends as much time talking as playing the guitar (in league with guitarists Frank Vignola and Lou Pallo, and bassist Nicki Parrott). It's like Paul is fronting his own talk show, dishing up double-entendres and reflecting on his days as an L.A. studio musician, telling tales on Bing Crosby. When a guest musician sits in, and sometimes very famous ones do, he finds every excuse to pick on them—an affectionate hazing that turns the subsequent performance into a dare and a gag. A few years ago, when one visitor reeled off a particularly splendid take on Django Reinhardt, Paul took a moment to illustrate how he'd come up with that particular method first, but then he delivers the punchline. He acts wounded: "You had to wait until I was 88 years old before you came over here to beat me up like that."

By the time the laughter subsides, the ensemble has jumped into something old and familiar—"Brazil" or "Sweet Georgia Brown" or "Tiger Rag"—and Paul shows everyone why, despite creaky joints, his name is literally synonymous with electric guitar.

ENZO'S JAZZ AT THE JOLLY HOTEL MADISON TOWERS

22 East 38th Street at Madison Avenue

☎ 212 802 0600

www.jollymadison.com/amenities_Enzo.htm

🚇 Grand Central 4/5/6

THERE'S NO OPERA BUFFO AT THIS ITALIAN BOUTIQUE HOTEL CALLED JOLLEY, BUT THERE IS JAZZ. Wednesdays and Fridays, Enzo's Jazz Room hosts two sets by notable players working the circuit. Vocalists have a plush platform, as the Midtown lounge vibe is ideal for piano trios and tours of the American songbook. Free antipasti comes with your $15 cover and one-drink minimum.

IRIDIUM

1650 Broadway at West 51st Street
☎ 212 582 2121 · www.iridiumjazzclub.com
🚇 49th Street N/R/W 50th Street 1

THIS BLUE-CHIP ROOM IS POISED AT A GLITTER-ING JUNCTURE. JUST A FEW BLOCKS NORTH OF Times Square, the view from its street-level entrance is a snapshot any tourist could love. Next door, vacationing Midwestern families join the singing waitrons at one of those faux-'50s diner-themed restaurants, belting out their own lullaby of Broadway.

Iridium fits the polished profile with both flash and substance. It's one of the few music establishments that mean it when it claims to serve food: pricey steaks and fancy Asian-themed appetizers, and a wine list you actually have to pause over. And while its new location (the club opened in 1994 across the block from Lincoln Center, but moved in 2001) lacks the interior pizzazz of the Gaudi-meets-Dr. Seuss original, this simple, two-tiered, blue-walled box of a space leaves little to focus on except the stage. The sound system was hand picked by Les Paul, who has held court every Monday night since 1995. Musically, the club books a much wider range of players than you might expect. Plenty of still-vital figures from a more golden jazz age—such as pianists Hank Jones, McCoy Tyner, and Andrew Hill, vibesman Bobby Hutcherson, and saxophonist Sam Rivers—check in for multi-night runs, something that keeps Iridium consistently on the map. That the venue also has lent a platform to the wizardly complexities of someone like Anthony Braxton, who led an ensemble of former students in an exploration of his "Ghost Trance Music" for an entire week in 2006, suggests the management is not just here for the tourist trade. Plenty of nights *are* about that, sure, but while no one was looking, Iridium has become an unexpected outpost of jazz's more eccentric thinkers.

JAZZ AT LINCOLN CENTER

Frederick P. Rose Hall

The Allen Room

Dizzy's Club Coca-Cola

☎ 212 258 9800 · www.jazzatlincolncenter.org

🚇 59th Street/Columbus Circle A/C/E/1/2/3

WHILE DEBATES OVER THE FUTURE OF JAZZ WILL SWIRL AS LONG AS THERE'S JAZZ TO argue about, there's no question that Jazz at Lincoln Center has been a focal point in the discussion. The institution, which rose to prominence through the 1990s as a platform for trumpeter and Pulitzer Prize-winning composer Wynton Marsalis, is all about putting jazz in an historical context. Basically, that means giving it the same treatment other art forms—such as classical music—get at Lincoln Center. Jazz repertory, a movement that has grown stronger as the last of the music's legendary performers begin to fade from view, is in the foreground here, with concert programs devoted to the music of pantheon figures such as Duke Ellington, John Coltrane, and Thelonious Monk, and a tightly rehearsed big band to tour the world playing their music. J@LC, as it is billed, isn't alone among non-profit organizations promoting jazz concert seasons in New York, or revisiting the classics, or even fostering new works by contemporary jazz composers (which it does as well). But it is the largest and most influential, thanks to artistic director Marsalis's user-friendly charisma, strong funding from public and private sources, and an uptown pedigree that takes jazz out of the smoky barroom environments that spawned it and into tonier realms more often occupied by operas and orchestras.

During the fall of 2004, J@LC finally abandoned its acoustically ill-suited base at Alice Tully Hall for what Marsalis calls the House of Swing: a dazzling new home on Columbus Circle. The main concert hall is named after Frederick P. Rose—the late real estate mogul who donated $10 million to the cause—and is contained within the 55-story, 2.77-million-square-foot Columbus Center, where Time-Warner is headquartered. It marks a Great Leap Forward for J@LC, which has dramatically increased its programming—by 100 percent, in fact—to keep three separate performance spaces going. The primary theater, Rose Hall, holds between 1,100 and 1,230 seats and emulates European opera house design, with an emphasis on an intimate feel even within a large space. A generous amount of vertical headroom—11 floors worth—makes triple-tiered seating possible, with only 80 feet separating the stage from the last, uppermost row. While the acoustics have been designed with jazz in mind, the room has proven highly adaptable: Even performances by chamber ensembles using complicated electronics translate beautifully. The architect, Rafael Viñoly, sought to collapse the traditional distance between performers and audience, which is more appropriate to the communal spirit of jazz. The nature of the acoustics, which was strongly influenced by Marsalis's input, is warmer and less echo-prone than what classical halls offer. "We're going for the clearest sound," Marsalis has said, "but with warm and golden overtones: golden, but not too dark."

Though the Rose offers ample wowzah (and ticket prices to match), J@LC's other two venues are even more charming. As performance spaces, they are at once high-end and full of character, something a first-time visitor might never anticipate given the visually noisy, urban mega-mall feel of the Columbus Circle entrance (well, it actually IS a mall) and the corporate museum sensibility that greets fresh arrivals at the elevators.

The Allen Room, a 300-600-seat space, offers an entirely different perspective, as its amphitheatre-style seating faces a 50-foot glass wall with a view of Central Park. Beyond the skyline panorama, the room's other big attraction is its modular nature. Jazz and dance can be integrated here in a way that hasn't been possible for J@LC before, with events focused on

Brazilian themes or swing dancing that feature professional dancers as well as opportunities for the audience to get out on the floor. Lincoln Center's venerable American Songbook series takes roost here, and that soaring view makes a perfect Manhattan backdrop for a singer at her piano: It's pure Woody Allen…or Berenice Abbott…or Charles Sheeler. Intimate and inviting as the Allen is, especially for such a large room, someone forgot to spend money on comfortable seating. The plastic and metal chairs were likely selected for convenience of storage, but in surroundings so otherwise posh, posteriors demand something even mildly padded.

Dizzy's is named in honor of Dizzy Gillespie and its carbonated corporate sponsor. The latter tribute is a sign of the times that rankles some purists but is of genuine consequence only to the most loyal of Pepsi drinkers. This is a singularly pleasing room in which to hear jazz. Partly, that's the luck of the skyline. The postcard view that wraps around behind the stage can't be topped (it's also a reminder that some of the city's important clubs are sequestered in basements, far from such luxuries). Dizzy's 140 seats fill a space encircled by smoothly curving wood panels that imply a kind of grotto, interrupted only by a large bar in one corner and swinging kitchen doors tucked away in another. Food and drink options are more than an afterthought (fried chicken and waffles, even), and while tickets are in the same range as other blue-chip venues, admission policies encourage a surprising number of students, leaned against side walls nursing their sodas. All this is more than enough to qualify Dizzy's as a date-night destination. What makes it a must is the chance to see some of the greatest performers in jazz do their thing amid the room's subdued glow and acoustic sparkle. Not every night can be as magic as one featuring 88-year-old Hank Jones playing effortless piano in a live recording session, but that's exactly what Dizzy's was made for.

The ongoing challenge for J@LC is to expand its reach to match the potential of its new home, which also includes a rehearsal and recording studio, a broadcast center, a classroom, and a jazz hall of fame named after the Ertegun family, founders of Atlantic Records. "We're trying to become as inclusive and broad-based a jazz-presenting organization as possible without watering down the artistic integrity of what we present," says artistic administrator Todd Barkan, who promises that "the sky's the limit." What that means, among other things, is that J@LC will continue to move in directions it's already been heading: further explorations of Afro-Cuban and Brazilian traditions and overlaps, for instance, and jazz orchestra tributes to musical giants who missed out during the organization's first decade. The current season includes an evening devoted to the music of Weather Report keyboardist Joe Zawinul—a seminal figure in the oft-scorned (by Marsalis himself) fusion movement of the 1970s— and a pair of composers who typically draw vehement rhetoric from J@LC consultant Stanley Crouch: pianist Cecil Taylor and saxophonist John Zorn. Maybe this is a simple matter of trying on some different hats to generate buzz. It suggests J@LC may not be entirely predictable. Barkan does not see his programs branching away from a foundation in swing-based jazz— an aesthetic the critic Albert Murray famously called "the velocity of celebration." He does promise "a little more imagination...You will see and hear all kinds of things."

52ND STREET

COMPARED TO THE MUCH-DIMINISHED STATE OF THE JAZZ LIFE IN MANHATTAN TODAY, THE glory days of 52nd Street—aka Swing Street—must strike some ardent fans like a fever dream. The street blossomed between the end of Prohibition and the societal shifts that came after World War II. It was all of two blocks, running between Fifth and Seventh Avenues. But the profusion of clubs that sprang up, drawing the greatest names in jazz, made it electric— the center of the universe for those who prized swing and, later, be-bop above all else.

The clubs, housed mostly in the unflattering brownstone basements of former speakeasies, sported evocative names: The Three Deuces, the Famous Door, the Spotlite, Jimmy Ryan's, the Onyx, the Yacht Club, Tondelayo's, Kelly's Stable, the Hickory House, the Carousel Club. William Gottlieb's famous photograph captures the scene around 1948: a riot of neon and names flashing from marquee banners, the colors reflecting off of puddles in a damp street. It looks like the promise New York City made to the imaginations of small-town radio listeners of the day, leaning forward to hear a saxophone leap through the airwaves, and dreaming of the night.

As historian Scott DeVeaux notes in his study, *The Birth of BeBop*, a wartime cabaret tax encouraged the booking of small instrumental groups, whose performances were exempt. Scarcely any important jazz artist missed an opportunity to play 52nd Street, whether it was Billie Holiday, Fats Waller, Coleman Hawkins, Dizzy Gillespie, Roy Eldridge, Lennie Tristano, Stuff Smith, Hot Lips Page, Charlie Parker, or Miles Davis.

Not that Davis seemed to care for it much. As DeVeaux quotes him, the trumpeter shuddered at his first glimpse of the Three Deuces in 1944: "It had such a big reputation in the jazz scene that I thought it would be all plush and shit. The bandstand wasn't nothing but a little tiny space that could hardly hold a piano. ...I remember thinking that it wasn't nothing but a hole in the wall."

Compare that to jazz impresario George Wein's recollection, who as a Boston high-schooler paid visits to his older brother Larry, who was studying at New York University. The pair would roam from 7 p.m. until daylight. Wein, thoroughly under age, would nurse a ginger ale at the bar to stretch his meager pocket change. "The highlight of the circuit was 52nd Street; it was one of heaven's avenues of gold," he writes in his autobiography, *Myself Among Others*. "...On a good night, you could walk into the Famous Door and see the whole Basie band crowded into the back of the room, swinging like mad."

Wein's avenue of gold wasn't paved so sweetly for very long. Gottlieb's photo seems to capture its high-flickering spirit just as its era was about to end. Strip clubs and such began to infiltrate, and the musical action was moving elsewhere. Even Charlie Parker had flown, a few blocks away, to lend his name to a new venue called Birdland. The bop era was in full fever, and Swing Street had swung its last.

JAZZ STANDARD

116 East 27th Street
between Park Avenue South & Lexington Avenue
☎ 212 576 2232 · www.jazzstandard.com
🚇 28th Street N/R/W/6

OH, THE CONUNDRUM OF THE JAZZ SUPPER CLUB! WHEN MUSIC ALONE WON'T MAKE A venue successful, the owner often decides to impose a menu and a drink minimum on patrons quite capable of burning their own mediocre cut of strip steak. And at a fraction of the price. Intrusive waitrons, ill-mannered diners smacking and slurping, the piercing jangle of cutlery—everything exists to distract you from the performers, who might as well return to the their long-forsaken Holiday Inn lounge gig. At least there they got some respect.

That's a worst-case scenario, of course, though the experience is not uncommon to dedicated clubgoers and unfortunate tourists. But never at the Jazz Standard, where the concept of pairing live jazz with what used to be called "fine dining" actually works. Part of that is some fundamental respect for the separation of church and state, as it were. The Standard, a 250-person capacity club, occupies a plush and roomy basement space below Blue Smoke, an expansive barbecue restaurant and bar. Patrons who want to chow down can stick to the upper level. Jazz (and sometimes world music) fans can settle in downstairs, but still enjoy tangy chicken wings, pulled pork sandwiches, or mac-and-cheese from a smaller, club-sized menu. Or not. This charmed resolution to an age-old problem can be attributed to Danny Meyer. The prize-winning chef and long-time jazz-lover got to realize two dreams in 2001, when he took over the Standard [and its sister enterprise, the restaurant 27 Standard] from his first cousin, who had opened the Rose Hill club four years earlier. Meyer finally got the barbecue house he'd always wanted, and he'd be able to indulge his jazz fandom on a first-person basis. He's managed to bring a casual big city sensibility to both. Designer Peter Bentel gave upstairs (more dramatic) and downstairs (more romantic) a look that emphasizes physical comfort—cushy red booths high enough to vanish into—and industrial-tech style. "It's an urban joint," says Meyer, who wants to convey a certain downhome folksy flavor while avoiding a bait 'n' tackle shop aesthetic. His advisors included documentarian Ken Burns (whose nearly 20 hours of "Jazz," put Louis Armstrong back on the charts again), who led Meyer to the photographer Charles Peterson, whose dozens of black-and-white images hang from the walls. The displays include many shots of jazz legends dressed to the nines for evenings of gourmandizing, babe-squeezing, and trading fours. Some of them are busy ripping through BBQ platters. One of pianist Thelonious Monk conveys a powerfully carnivorous mood: The brilliantly eccentric composer looks snazzy in his suit with the broad "Mr. B" lapels, staring with demonic focus at a pile of slaughtered ribs gathered in his plate. Smoke curls upward from the cigarette between his fingertips.

"There's an inviting vibe about the place," says bassist and composer Ben Allison, part of a new generation of performers who have made the Standard a hub, often premiering new tunes, trying out new ensembles, or hosting weeklong festivals. The venue frequently presents players from Allison's non-profit Jazz Composer's Alliance, and is a favorite spot for Palmetto Records, a top independent jazz label, to showcase artists' works-in-progress—as it did when renascent 1960s pianist Andrew Hill was prepping his big band for a recording session. "There's excellent sound. And the people who work there are very accommodating. The management is glad to see you. I'm not naming names, but jazz clubs are notorious for rude owners, and bad staffs that act too cool for the customers."

Since the Standard occupies a geographic middle ground between clubs uptown (conventionally, more geared to the tourist trade) and downtown (aggressively hip holes-in-the-wall), its bookings draw from the best of both worlds, which automatically makes the venue more progressive than most of its competition (which is to say, places with carpeting and a decent wine selection). It's distinguished, as well, by an earlier start time (the first set is at 7:30 p.m.) and the abolition of the dreaded drink minimum, which usually runs $10. "I'd like to make jazz relevant to more people more of the time," says Meyer, a former jazz DJ in college who recalls welling up with tears immediately after reopening the Standard, when the South African pianist Abdullah Ibrahim headlined. "It feels like the jazz world can be too literate for its own good. I mean, why does everyone look at you like you're nuts when you say you're going to open up a jazz club?"

JAZZ AT
ST. PETER'S CHURCH

619 Lexington Avenue at East 54th Street

☎ 212 935 2200 · www.saintpeters.org

🚊 Lexington Avenue E/V, 51st Street 6

JAZZ MUSICIANS GO OUT SWINGING. THEY REALLY DO: THIS VERY MODERN MODEL OF A LUTHERAN church has been the site of countless memorial services for performers both beloved and bedeviled since the mid-1960s, when the late Rev. John Garcia Gensel initiated a jazz ministry here. The occasions, though sad, are so celebratory that it's hard not to go home without a tear in your eye and a song in your heart. Peers gather for unique performances to send off their former bandmates, and the tribute concerts can go on for two or three hours. When the deceased is someone who has altered jazz history—like Sun Ra, or the brilliant New Orleans drummer Ed Blackwell—the stage overflows with musical eulogists of equally legendary repute. And, yes, that was Abbey Lincoln dishing up sweet potatoes in the potluck line outside the auditorium.

But you don't have to wait for a funeral to enjoy jazz at St. Peter's. The church offers concerts several times a week, including a Wednesday lunch series, a Sunday vespers program, and outdoor performances on its adjacent plaza.

THE KITANO

66 Park Avenue at East 38th Street

☎ 212 885 7000

🚇 Grand Central 4/5/6

THIS ELEGANT JAPANESE HOTEL SITS ON THE DOWNTOWN FLIPSIDE OF THE OLD PAN AM BUILD-ing. There's no reason to notice it. Walk inside, however, and the thoughtful design—you might think you're inside a Bento box, albeit one decorated with Botero sculptures—is inviting. Upstairs from the lobby is a small bar that has lately evolved into one of the city's real insider spots. Thanks to Juinichi Kasaga, a jazz-loving manager who doubles as a booker, the hotel now hosts bands Wednesdays through Sundays. Kasaga, whose gentle manner can't contain his enthusiasm for the music, has a specific focus. He's a recovering fan of Bradley's, the vintage bar near NYU that was shuttered in the late 1990s, dispatching many fans and musicians into sackcloth-and-ashes despair. There will never be another place like it, and its reverse L-shaped space with the piano in the crook before the dogleg into the kitchen. Everyone who became anyone in more-or-less mainstream New York jazz cut their teeth at Bradley's, or lost them.

The Kitano can't really recapture that. What it does is feature quartets and quintets, generally, that need a piano like they had at Bradley's. In fact, no band without a pianist will get booked. Makes life simple. Kasaga, who has a touch of one of Haruki Murakami's jazz-loving everymen about him, has great ears. He loves noted vets, but will just as often feature some of the hottest younger players on the scene. Someone like tenor saxophonist Donny McCaslin, whose sound can really grab someone's collar when they're sitting a couple of arm-lengths away, a vantage point that is among the chief reasons for visiting the Kitano.

SWING 46

349 West 46th Street
between Eighth & Ninth Avenues
☎ 212 262 9554 · www.swing46.com
🚇 42nd Street A/C/E

AMECCA FOR DANCERS WHO WANT TO RELIVE THE GLORY DAYS OF BIG BAND SWING, THIS stylish supper club boasts big bands or smaller combos every night. The music summons earlier jazz eras, implied by names of such revivalist crews as The Tiger Town Five and the Crescent City Maulers. Its calendar also has room for more contemporary outfits: J.C. Hopkins's whimsical Biggish Band holds forth here on occasions, with the spotlight focused on Queen Esther, a blues-steeped vocalist who commands the house with ease and more than a touch of old-school sass. And though the term "swing" alludes primarily to the 1930s dance style, it can also incorporate other permutations. Try to catch Jimmy "Preacher" Robins when he has a set. The natural-born extrovert whips up a Harlem groove on the Hammond B-3 organ—once the very soul of every little bar in African-American neighborhoods nationwide, and an instrument that has become steadily more in vogue again as a new generation of jam bands rediscover the fundamental good times inherent in its warm, churchy grooves. Plus, anyone can dance to it, an imperative for up to 100 smooth steppers a show at Swing 46.

ZANKEL HALL

57th Street at Seventh Avenue

☎ 212 247 7800 · www.carnegiehall.org

🚇 Columbus Circle A/B/C/D/1 57th Street N/Q/R/W

🚇 Seventh Avenue D/E

BEFORE IT REOPENED AS ZANKEL HALL IN SEPTEMBER 2003, THE BASEMENT AUDITORIUM at Carnegie Hall had been through several incarnations. Most notably, starting around 1895, it was known for a half-century as the Carnegie Lyceum, across whose stage trod Spencer Tracy, Kirk Douglas, and Edward G. Robinson. Later, it was the Carnegie Playhouse, and then, in 1960, it became a cinema, eventually leased to a corporate entity and, by 1997, suddenly vacant for the first time in a century.

Now, it's a 600-seat hall, accessible via an escalator that takes you into an exterior that feels ceremonial: A gold-tinted convex wall defines the theater, inviting a gentle rub of the hand, as if encountering an alien temple on some "Star Trek" offshoot. The programs explore musical arcs almost as far-flung, both as a landing strip for African and Asian musicians making their New York tour stops, and in the sense of sonic explorations. The venue has an ongoing relationship with Nonesuch Records, whose artists frequently grace the stage, as well as the chamber music rebels Bang on a Can.

Jazz has an enviable platform here. Brad Mehldau, Joshua Redman, Bill Frisell, Fred Hersch, and Omar Sosa, among others, have headlined in the past few years. While Carnegie Hall itself has an historic role in the history of jazz—and nearly every other kind of American music—Zankel offers a somewhat more niche-driven, boutique experience. The fact that the room's designers decided to pattern the cherry-lined décor after George Nelson's famous 1950s bench doesn't hurt one bit.

WOODY ALLEN

CAFÉ CARLYLE

35 East 76th Street
between Madison & Park Avenues
☎ 212 570 7189
🚇 77th Street 6

MUCH AS, SAY, A VISIT TO THE STATUE OF LIB-
ERTY, OR AFTERNOON MUNCHING HOT DOGS
in the cheap seats at Yankee Stadium, there are specific
sights and experiences that are quintessentially New
York. The place would be a little less fun—and a lot
less New York—without them. Look at Woody Allen.
He's pulling a double shift, even. The guy who made
Manhattan, and a score of other cinematic valentines
to the city, has done more than any other filmmaker
besides Martin Scorsese to define his hometown on the
big screen. Yet, as much as he loves New York, he also
loves jazz. He loves old-time jazz, and he plays it every
Monday night. He loves playing it so much he skipped
the Oscars in 1978—the year *Annie Hall* swept the
awards—because he didn't want to miss his weekly
gig at Michael's Pub. These days, the engagement is at
Café Carlyle, in the posh Upper East Side hotel, where
the late Bobby Short made himself a legend. Mondays
belong to Allen and a small group of musicians who
play New Orleans-style jazz from the 1920s and '30s.
There's not much fuss. Allen wanders in from a door
at the end of the bar, settles at a table with his wife,
Soon-Yi Previn, and their guests, opens up an instrument case, and begins to assemble his clarinet. That's
about as good as it gets for the celebrity gawk factor
(unless, of course, that really is Peter Boyle sitting at
their table, but the jury never reaches a verdict). Soon,
the Woodman is on stage with his cohorts. He looks
his age, 71, his nose offering a familiar perch for those
signature glasses, with their thick black frames. Eddy
Davis, a banjo player whose endeavors include some-

thing called The New York Society for the Preservation of Illegitimate Music, handles the arrangements. There's also a piano, drums, trumpet, trombone, and bass, with everyone—except Woody—pitching in on vocals. The music is the kind that Jelly Roll Morton and Louis Armstrong would have been conversant in, with selections like "Wild Man Blues" and "Dippermouth Blues," that are directly associated with them. The performances are jaunty and casually askew, making the most of the tunes' antique charms. Allen's no virtuoso, but he plays with focus and panache. The master of this form is a clarinet player named Ken Peplowski, who can sweep fluidly into the upper ranges, and target tricky notes with a piercing attack. But the setting, which feels an awful lot like a scene in a Woody Allen film, doesn't call for such intensity. It's still spirited, which the music demands, but mellow enough not to rattle the mood of diners sipping on $20 cocktails. The intimacy of the room allows the music to breathe naturally, and if you're occupying one of the cheap seats ($40 scores a barstool), you'll be leaning forward once in a while to catch a stray lyric (or crane your neck around one of the persistent shutterbugs who take photos throughout the hour-long show).

As New York rituals go, it's surprisingly cool. And Allen proves accommodating and gracious after he finishes off the night with a short trio set. A small crowd trails him out the exit door and into a hallway where he shyly dispenses autographs and receives the arms of strangers who pull him close, grinning for flashbulbs.

CLEOPATRA'S NEEDLE • 100

MAKOR • 101

SMOKE • 102

TRIAD THEATRE • 104

CLEOPATRA'S NEEDLE

2485 Broadway between West 92nd &
West 93rd Streets

☎ 212-769-6969 · www.cleopatrasneedleny.com

🚇 96th Street 1/2/3

THE REAL CLEOPATRA'S NEEDLE IS AN ANCIENT OBELISK THAT NOW RESIDES ON THE THAMES Embankment in London, where it's been since 1879—a long, long way from Heliopolis, where the Pharoah Thothmes III erected it around 1,500 BC. A second "needle" sits near East Drive at East 82nd Street, gifted by Egypt to New York City in 1881.

A neighborhood jazz hangout not far from Columbia University, this place—yet another Needle—can't claim such totemic antiquity. Sheesh. The moniker is simply a tip that its kitchen serves Middle Eastern fare. It's also one of the more musician-friendly rooms in town, particularly hospitable to students from the nearby Julliard and Manhattan Schools of Music, and jam session regulars who come by for the Monday night sessions overseen by pianist Eric Lewis.

MAKOR

35 West 67th Street
Between Central Park West & Columbus Avenue
☎ 212 601 1000 · www.makor.org
🚇 66th Street 1

TRULY A PHENOMENON OF THE UPPER WEST SIDE: THE NON-PROFIT CULTURAL CENTER AS singles meet-and-greet. Founded by philanthropist Michael Steinhardt in 1999, Makor occupies a five-story, 22,000-square-foot house that was built in 1904 and originally served as a residence for elderly Swiss women. In 2001, Steinhardt donated the $16 million property to the 92nd Street Y, which now operates its various facilities (which include a screening room, art gallery, gym, and classrooms). The downstairs performance space and bar draws scenesters in their 20s and 30s who know from Prada and don't mind a little high art with their cocktails. The emphasis is on Jewish cultural offerings—everything from klezmer to Kinky (Friedman)—and the bookings are sharp enough to lure Rockport-shod downtowners onto the 1 line for a look-see.

They'll find it's worth the jaunt, as the space is designed to maximize views of the stage, with the bar situated well behind the booths and tables in the main seating area. Jazzier headliners have included Norah Jones—who enjoyed a pre-fame residency here—Kenny Garrett, Charlie Hunter, Bobby Watson, Marc Ribot, Anthony Coleman, James Carter, Leon Parker, Fred Hersch, Soulive, Christian McBride, Perry Robinson, and the Jazz Mandolin Project. Not bad, especially within spitting distance of the Café des Artistes and Central Park.

SMOKE

2751 Broadway at West 105th Street

☎ 212 864 6622 · www.smokejazz.com

🚇 103rd Street 1

THOUGH IT IS SOMETHING LIKE THE HOLY LAND TO (JERRY) SEINFELDIANS, AND STOMPING grounds for generations of Columbia students, the Upper West Side isn't the first stop that comes to mind on anyone's jazz itinerary. A few blocks up and over, there's Harlem, which boasts not only its resonant history but the kind of after-hours haunts that continue to bring that history to life. A short ride down Broadway brings you first to Jazz at Lincoln Center. Then, to a hub of "uptown" venues that faintly echo the vitality of a classic era amid the neon ruckus of the new Times Square. So there's no reason to expect any revelations in a part of town so thoroughly out-jazzed by its adjacent precincts.

Yet, that's what makes Smoke even more special. This venue's name evokes jazz iconography. Think of photographer Herman Leonard, whose black-and-white portraits of legends like Billie Holiday and Lester Young were typically cloaked in a halo of cigarette smoke. And it also reflects an aficionado's most approving verb: When the musicians smoke on the bandstand, it doesn't get any better. Ironic, then, that mayoral maneuvers have banned tobacco use, even in small bars such as this, which thrive on a kind of intimacy and atmosphere that evokes another time. But those qualities, at least, never go out of style, and Smoke rises to the occasion. Catching a late night set here feels the way you always imagined a Gotham jazz hang should. That's especially true on weekends, when the bookings tap the frontlines of hard-bop veterans and adroit newbies, name attractions who don't usually play clubs this small. Since the room only holds about 75 people, the Steinway grand piano sounds as clear from the far end of the vintage long bar as it does at one of the tightly clustered tables nestled at the lip of the stage. And since the décor suggests that of an agreeably distressed bordello—burgundy velvet drapes, faux tin ceiling, mahogany wood, aged brick walls, and a handcrafted banquette whose cushions whisper of date-night indulgence—it's easy to forget that you're in post-millennial Manhattan. When the alto saxophonist calls an old Charlie Parker tune, and bites into it fast with a flurry of fingertips and harmonic wizardry, the only time that really matters is the rhythm spilling out from the drum kit. But the truth is, even though Smoke is one of the city's newest jazz clubs—it opened in 1999—it's actually been around much longer. Before bartenders Paul Stache and Frank Christopher bought the place and refurbished it, the joint enjoyed a 22-year run as Augie's Jazz Bar. Its owner, who owns the unforgettable name of Augustus Quertas, ran it more like a social club than a business, cultivating the sort of loyal clientele whose collective affection for the barkeep's idiosyncrasies guaranteed him status as a local legend. Some of the keenest talents of a current generation of jazz artists, including pianists Brad Mehldau and Jackie Terrasson, started out at Augie's—and still visit Smoke, either to headline or to hang out. Another regular, back during his Columbia days, was the novelist and screenwriter Paul Auster, who paid his regards by immortalizing the still-quite-mortal Augie. Auster gave his name, and life story, to Harvey Keitel's rascal philsopher-cum-tobacco-vendor in—what else?—*Smoke*.

TRIAD THEATRE

158 West 72nd Street
between Broadway & Columbus Avenue
☎ 212 362 2590 · www.triadnyc.com
🚇 72nd Street 1/2/3

TWO VENUES IN ONE, THE TRIAD CONSISTS OF A SMALL, STREET-LEVEL BAR (THE DARK STAR Lounge) with a stage just big enough to welcome a drum kit for some combo action, and an upstairs cabaret-style theater with cocktail table seating on the floor and a steeply pitched balcony above. Theatrical productions fill the calendar, with jazz performances as a sidebar. That means lots of vocalists, as befits the venue's overall bent for off-Broadway musicals, but also Latin jazz and even some avant-garde. The room holds about 130 patrons, which makes it comfortable and intimate. Check the website for music listings.

LENOX LOUNGE • 108
MINTON'S PLAYHOUSE • 114
SHOWMAN'S CAFE • 117
ST. NICK'S PUB • 118

HARLEM

LENOX LOUNGE

288 Lenox Avenue at West 125th Street
☎ 212 427 0253 · www.lenoxlounge.com
🚇 125th Street 2/3

HARLEM MAY BE ENJOYING ITS SECOND RE-
NAISSANCE. ONLY A FEW YEARS AGO, THOSE
Strivers Row brownstones were one of Manhattan's
sweetest real estate bargains. But prices have jumped.
Former president Bill Clinton keeps his office in the
neighborhood. Yet, it's still hard to find a cab after
dark. Such is prosperity. It's a different kind of hey-
day than was first associated with these broad-shoul-
dered blocks—originally a Dutch settlement that was
almost exclusively white and fancy until the first years
of the 20th century. African-Americans began pouring into the neighborhood in greater numbers after a
1904 real estate collapse and by 1920 had established
a dominant community, eclipsing dwindling popula-
tions of Eastern European Jews and Italians who had
briefly settled there.

During the 1920s and '30s, Harlem became a platform for the emergence of a new African-American
consciousness in the arts. This vibrancy was shared by
jazz of the period: in the eruptive improvising genius
of Louis Armstrong, for instance, and in the conta-
gious zest of Duke Ellington's Jungle Band, which
reigned at the Cotton Club.

That era abides, if only in the sepia-toned rev-
erie of Ken Burns documentaries and the jazz repertory movement championed by Wynton Marsalis and
Jazz at Lincoln Center. It's history. Somehow, though,
you can feel its authentic spark flickering at the Lenox
Lounge. The club, which was built in 1939, is a gem:
the last of the Art Deco bars in the city. Thanks to a
$450,000 loan from the Upper Manhattan Empower-
ment Zone, the Lenox Lounge was restored in 2000,
so that the way it looks now is as close as possible to

the way it looked then. Romare Bearden and James Baldwin once were in the house. So were Malcolm X and Langston Hughes. True, Billie Holiday no longer sits at her table—first one on the left—in the Zebra Room, which occupies the rear of the club, and is so named for its zebra-patterned wallpaper. There's a story behind the wallpaper, too: Seems the owners of a rival club, the El Morocco, didn't appreciate the lounge emulating *its* zebra theme, and initiated a dispute that kept the Lenox from opening until 1942.

Originally one of the Harlem clubs that presented black entertainers for exclusively white audiences, the lounge now draws all kinds of attention, much of it driven by nostalgia for an era of uptown sophistication. The venue's vintage design is irresistible to contemporary celebrities and filmmakers. Everyone likes to use the club for a backdrop, whether in the Samuel L. Jackson remake of *Shaft* or for retro fashion shoots.

Despite the high style, the Lenox is very much a neighborhood bar. Live music here, which is not exclusively jazz, is the preserve of the Zebra Room, for which there is a cover charge. Often, there's a wholly different crowd listening in back than is drinking up front. The bar attracts a crosssection of patrons that is pure New York: plenty of Asian and European tourists, students over from nearby Columbia University, characters from around the block, and dandies from the day, sage-like jazz aficionados who can tell you like it is—or was—and musicians chilling out before or after a set.

Patience Higgins is chief among them. The Harlem mainstay leads his Sugar Hill Quartet every Monday night. Higgins burns up the hard-bop canon, playing Sonny Rollins ("St. Thomas"), John Coltrane ("Mr. P.C."), and Kenny Dorham ("Blue Bossa"). He draws on decades of touring and recording, including stints with rhythm-and-blues titans Wilson Pickett and Sam and Dave, and boasts an extroverted style customized for these occasions. Higgins is a dapper gent who loves to improvise like a stand-up comedian. He may launch into a spontaneous diatribe against the evils of Kenny G. "It's not jazz, it's pop! Say it!" he'll beseech, and have the tightly packed crowd rally in unison: "Pop!" When he plays an extended version of Marvin Gaye's "What's Goin' On?" he might veer into politics, denouncing the Republican agenda with a humorously verbose fervor that prompts laughter and cheers. Is Bill Clinton in the house?

If so, it would not be unusual. Impromptu guests have included the rare Rock and Roll Hall of Famer (Lou Reed, who has a keen ear for jazz trumpeters, sat in one night with a band), as well as players stepping out of the Jazz at Lincoln Center orbit, such as pianist Eric Reed, and the exceptional trombonist, Wycliffe Gordon. Ya never know, as Holiday once sang, what a little moonlight can do.

HISTORIC HARLEM

HARLEM THEN AND HARLEM NOW MEANS TWO VASTLY DIFFERENT THINGS WHEN IT COMES to jazz. Although the Apollo Theater, which was refurbished and reopened in 1985 and now is owned by the State of New York, abides as a symbol of Harlem's past and present, it does so in a different context than in 1934, when its first amateur night lured hopefuls to the corner of 125th Street and Lenox Avenue. The 90-year-old structure, now managed as a non-profit and accorded historic landmark status, is a wonderful urban museum piece: the place for televised concert specials and awards ceremonies. Its revitalization speaks to the promise of an emerging Harlem of the 21st century, but it also stands as a nostalgic monument to the Harlem that was.

And yet, Harlem nostalgia is nothing new. More than 40 years ago, novelist and critic Ralph Ellison was already memorializing a time, a place and a sound that was seminal to this neighborhood:

"It was itself a texture of fragments, repetitive, nervous, not fully formed; its melodic lines underground, secret and taunting; its riffs jeering—'Salt peanuts! Salt peanuts!'—its timbres flat or shrill, with a minimum of thrilling vibrato. Its rhythms were out of stride and seemingly arbitrary, its drummers frozen-faced introverts dedicated to chaos."

Ellison, writing in the January 1959 issue of *Esquire*, was describing "the rumpus at Minton's." As in Minton's Playhouse, a bar and music room that occupied the ground floor of the Cecil Hotel, at 210 West 118th Street. The rumpus was be-bop, or bop, "hardly more than a nonsense syllable," yet the term that would become most associated with the revolutionary sound birthed at Minton's in the early 1940s. Kenny Clarke, who redesigned the DNA of jazz drumming, was the linchpin of the house band. A then-unknown Thelonious Monk was the pianist. That's him, smiling broadly, in William Gottlieb's 1947 photograph, sharp in pinstripes, beret, and sunglasses, standing by the Minton's awning with some formidable company: trumpeters Howard McGhee and Roy Eldridge, and Teddy Hill, the tenor saxophonist and bandleader who managed the club. Dizzy Gillespie and Charlie Parker (upon arriving in New York in 1942) were mainstays, cooking up a brisk and bold new music in after-hours jam sessions. Charlie Christian, the legendary guitarist who brought the instrument out of the background and into the spotlight of jazz improvisation, found a home at Minton's and played there frequently. Lore has it that, though ailing from tuberculosis, Christian would rise from his sickbed, sneak over to the club, and play in the weeks before his untimely death, at age 25, in 1942.

Minton's provided an outlet, a safe harbor for musicians to visit on an off-night—Mondays, the place was filled with band and cast members from the Apollo Theatre, who came for a free meal and stuck around to jam—or to develop new tricks away from the particular rigors of the big band. "We invented our own way of getting from one place to the next," is how Gillespie described it in his memoir, *To Be or Not To Bop*. And while Minton's was scarcely alone among significant Harlem nightspots—Monroe's Uptown House lays claim to a similar history—it occupies a mythic place in jazz lore. Efforts by entrepreneurs (including Robert De Niro) to reestablish Minton's came to naught, until April 2006 when the bar was renovated and reopened by Earl Spain, the former owner of popular Harlem night spot St. Nick's Pub (see page TK).

Equally as mythic was The Cotton Club—celebrated in Francis Ford Coppola's 1984 movie—which opened in 1923 at the Lenox Avenue site of the former Club Deluxe, which had been owned by Jack Johnson, the heavyweight boxing champ. The club, where top black entertainers played, sang, and danced for exclusively white audiences, was the brainchild of a mobster, Owney Madden. Back on the streets after an eight-year stint at Sing Sing, the convicted murderer needed an outlet to safely sell his beer despite Prohibition. The Cotton Club proved ideal, and not only for the bootleg business. The fancy showplace was pivotal in the career of Duke Ellington, whose orchestra held sway six nights a week between 1927 and 1931. Subsequent bandleaders included Cab Calloway and Jimmie Lunceford. The Cotton Club's reign was cut short in 1936 when racial discord made Harlem less secure for the venue's free-spending white patrons. The club closed, and opened on West 48th Street, where it lasted another four years.

The 1930s Swing Era was epitomized by another fabled venue: The Savoy Ballroom. The massive dancehall sprawled across an entire block between 140th and 141st Streets along Lenox Avenue. Opening in 1926, the Savoy became the land of a thousand dances, a racially integrated club that fostered crazes such as the Lindy Hop and the Big Apple. The following January, drummer Chick Webb began performing with his orchestra there, and became a sensation. Webb, a hunchback whose growth was stunted by spinal tuberculosis, led his musicians from a center-stage platform where he sat behind a customized kit that included a 28-inch kick drum. He did not have the kind of star soloists that other big bands claimed, but he did make a major discovery: A 17-year-old orphan named Ella Fitzgerald. She joined the band in 1934, launching one of jazz's greatest careers. Webb achieved two pinnacles in 1937 and 1938, when he trumped the groups of Benny Goodman and Count Basie in respective battles of the bands. His 1939 death left Fitzgerald in charge of the band, but the Swing Era had already begun its slow fade. Though the Savoy remained in business until 1958, it was, by then, the vestige of yet another phase in the history of jazz and of Harlem.

MINTON'S PLAYHOUSE

206-210 West 118th Street at Adam Clayton Powell/
Seventh Avenue and St. Nicholas Avenue

☎ 212 864 8346

🚇 116th Street 2/3/C

SOMETHING LIKE THE LOS ALAMOS OF BEBOP,
MINTON'S WAS THE LABORATORY WHERE JAZZ
went nuclear in the 1940s (see page TK). The historic
venue sat closed for decades, but finally returned in
April 2006. "We just ran across it," explains Celeste
Sapp, the no-nonsense woman who runs the sizable bar
along with Earl Spain, the former owner of another
Harlem staple, St. Nick's Pub. Spain was looking for a
new venue when he left St. Nick's after 15 years. And
when he found it, says Sapp, he wanted to have "the
longest bar in Harlem."

Funding came together and he got that bar—and
Minton's with it, accomplishing what numerous other
speculators had failed to do: Reopen what may be
Manhattan's most celebrated jazz site. The bar, which
Spain had designed and installed as part of a gut renovation that ran beyond $300,000, stretches from just
inside the door to a few feet before the bandstand in
an extremely deep, rectangular space. "The floor felt
like you were going to fall through it. It did!" Sapp
exclaims. "It was nothing but a shell."

Now it's one of the spiffier places to hear jazz in
Harlem. The layout is basic, but the sparkly tile floor
space is roomy enough for dancing, and the neon sig-
nage that announces "M-I-N-T-O-N-S-P-L-A-Y-H-O-
U-S-E" appears to be doing a jitterbug, with letters
tilted playfully to either side.

Bands play every night, attracting a friendly local
crowd—this is the kind of spot where women still
wear blossoms in their hair, and men know how to
rock a Kangol—and Japanese tourists who sit rapt in
front of the stage with identical pink umbrella drinks.

Sometimes, residents of the adjacent Cecil Hotel, now a city-owned property that caters to the elderly, drop by. "There's this man named Mr. Robinson who lives in Miles Davis's old room," Sapp says. "This cat tells me stories every day about this and about that. There's not anything that he doesn't know."

He may soon get a chance to share that lore with an audience. Sapp hopes to have a Minton's Reunion sometime in the immediate future. As bandleader Eli Fontaine, a gregarious regular on the premises, likes to say: "Come and get a piece of history."

JAZZ MUSEUM IN HARLEM

104 East 126th Street Suite 2D
between Park and Lexington Avenues
☎ 212 348 8300 · www.jazzmuseuminharlem.org
🚇 Lexington Avenue 4/5/6

NOT A MUSEUM IN PHYSICAL FACT YET, THE JAZZ MUSEUM OF HARLEM IS AN ACTIVE PRO-ducer of historical programs and concerts that draw attention to Harlem's significance in shaping jazz. Events, like the popular "Harlem Speaks" series, are staged at the museum's offices or at satellite locations, such as the Rubin Museum of Art (150 West 17th Street; 212 620 5000), which also hosts frequent concerts. The museum was founded in 2002 by Leonard Garment, a saxophonist and jazz enthusiast who more notoriously served as special counsel to Richard Nixon during the turbulent final two years of his presidency. (Garment also is the author of *In Search of Deep Throat: The Greatest Political Mystery of Our Time*, in which he revealed—incorrectly, it turned out—the identity of the Watergate source). As the search continues for a home, the museum has evolved into one of the best resources for the music's living history.

SHOWMAN'S CAFE

375 West 125th Street Between St. Nicholas
& Morningside Avenues
☎ 212 864 8941
🚇 125th Street A/B/C/D

BACK WHEN IT FIRST OPENED, IN 1947, THIS NIGHTSPOT WAS ADJACENT TO THE APOLLO Theater, whose entertainers considered the bar and restaurant their "living room." Showman's didn't become a music venue until 1978, and when it did, the sound was organized around a Hammond B-3 organ—the bedrock of groove-based black nightclub music, as epitomized by the likes of Jimmy Smith, Jack McDuff, and Charles Earland (and sampled on many a Beastie Boys 45). The club was forced to relocate, to Frederick Douglass Boulevard, after a 1985 fire, but owner Al Howard has persistently kept the faith. A 30-plus year veteran of the New York City Police Department, Howard was a supervisor of detectives chasing down the "Son of Sam" in 1977. But he nearly lost his bar in 1997, amid redevelopment plans for the Harlem USA urban mall. A new partner joined him, and Showman's reopened the next year at its current address.

The organ continues to reign supreme at Showman's, which features neighborhood jazz fixtures every night but Sunday, when it lures bigger names to its bandstand. The club, which can accommodate about 100 patrons, does little to draw attention to itself, but creates an amiable environment for anyone who enjoys a home-style neighborhood jam—with a shot of whisky on the side.

ST. NICK'S PUB

773 St. Nicholas Avenue at West 149th Street

☎ 212 283 9728

🚇 145th Street A/B/C/D

NO. 1 WITH A BULLET AMONG EUROPEAN TOURISTS SCOPING OUT THEIR AUTHENTIC HARLEM jazz experience, this downstairs bar a few blocks up from the 145th Street subway—where, yes, you can take the A train—is also a good bet for those who don't have to sweat the exchange rate. The cover charge is only $3, and even that includes a piece of fried chicken with rice delivered to your table—if you ask nicely.

Mondays are devoted to late-night jam sessions, a Harlem tradition and prime time to drop in. No matter who you are, you won't feel self-conscious. Audiences are conspicuously multilingual, as St. Nick's is a primary stop on many Harlem bus tours so popular with Europeans and Asians. But the neighborhood folks are just as present, whether knocking back a whiskey at the bar, carrying on an intense conversation with a table of first-time visitors, or squeezing their way across the floor to answer a pay phone that inexplicably rings on the wall near the bandstand. One regular, an older man dressed to the nines in a white suit and bowler hat, sits in the corner near the entrance, smiling quietly behind pitch-black shades. Before the night is done, the bandleader will announce him as the winner of the "best-dressed man in Harlem" contest, and Mr. Gene Davis will be onstage, belting out a blues number. St. Nick's is famous for its jam sessions, which attract seasoned musicians (such as cornetist Olu Dara, who lives nearby) and sacrificial newbies game for a few competitive choruses. But, really, the show is always on. This bar used to be known as the Lucky Rendezvous, and the sense of fortunate adventure that implies continues to hold true.

GOSPEL BRUNCHES

PRAISE THE LORD AND PASS THE GRAVY. MUCH IN KEEPING WITH THE SOUTHERN TRADITION OF massive potluck spreads served picnic-style on church lawns after a long-winded morning service, the Harlem gospel brunch brings it all back home. This is true, even for secular humanists who have never dipped below the Mason-Dixon Line. Restaurants across Harlem open their doors on late Sunday mornings to accommodate thousands of hungry worshippers flooding out of services on the church-crowded blocks. Not all offer live music, but for those who like to stay in the spirit—or simply savor another aspect of Harlem culture—the gospel brunch can fill both the belly and the soul.

Some notable brunch options:

COPELAND'S
547 West 145th Street
between Broadway & Amsterdam Avenue
☎ 212 234 2357
🚇 145th Street 1

COTTON CLUB
656 West 125th Street at Riverside Drive
☎ 212 663 7980 · www.cottonclub-newyork.com
🚇 125th Street 1

LONDEL'S SUPPER CLUB
2620 Frederick Douglass Boulevard
between West 139th & West 140th Streets
☎ 212 234 6114
🚇 135th Street B/C

BROWNSTONES, BISCUITS, & BEBOP

HARLEM JAZZ STROLLS

☎ 718 680 6677 · www.SwingStreets.com

HARLEM, IN SO MANY WAYS, EVOKES THE GHOSTS OF JAZZ PAST. THE NEIGHBORHOOD IS experiencing a welcome (from most vantage points) millennial shift, as business investments and a surge in real estate sales have begun to make the classic, far-uptown locale a newly desirable destination. So, perhaps, the promise of jazz future abides here as well. But, sadly, many of the historic jazz sites that put Harlem on the cultural map no longer exist. Hot spots such as the Savoy Ballroom and the original Cotton Club are long vanished. Vacant lots and bland urban shopping strips have taken their place, with a plaque stuck somewhere nearby to commemorate that which swung.

That's one of the more poignant aspects of Paul Blair's Sunday morning Harlem jazz walks. The Brooklyn-based journalist and historian actually leads three different tours of Harlem, as well as strolls through Midtown, Greenwich Village, and the East Village, each glancing back at the comings and goings of jazz greats and great jazz venues. Blair's an affable sort who manages to reel off all sorts of minutiae without losing his audience. His original tour, titled "Brownstones, Biscuits and Bebop" covers central Harlem, with a casual amble over a nearly 20-block area beginning at 125th Street and Lenox Avenue and heading north, with particular attention paid to the streets between Lenox and Seventh Avenue. Particularly fun is the walk down a block (West 133rd Street), that once was so thick with after-hours joints and basement clubs that it was called Jungle Alley. A litany of club names sounds like nothing so much as stray lyrics from an old blues song: The Nest, Basement Brownie's, Mother Shepherd's, Tillie's Chicken Shack, Pod and Jerry's Log Cabin, Mexico's. That was in the 1920s and '30s. The thing is, the street is still jumping. Only, at noontime on Sunday, the music pouring out of so many doors—even amplified through cheap speakers propped on porch steps—is gospel: fiery, foot-stomping, house-rocking gospel. It's a resonant reminder of the dualities of Harlem musical life, and the rituals that define Saturday night and Sunday morning.

Blair also is good on the "Fats Waller slept here" details. You will learn, for instance, that Jelly Roll Morton lived at 209 West 131st between Seventh and Frederick Douglass avenues. That Langston Hughes spent two decades on the block of West 127th Street at Fifth Avenue. That Roy Campanella sold liquor from a storefront at West 134th Street and Seventh Avenue, above the long-gone Clark Monroe's Uptown House—one of the seedbeds of bebop.

The tours come complete with an annotated homemade CD, which features relevant tracks: Cab Calloway vamping his way through a 1942 version of "I Get the Neck of the Chicken" or "Jumpin' at the Woodside," a 1938 tune, played by Count Basie's band (with Lester Young on tenor), and named after the hotel on Seventh Avenue near West 142nd Street. By the time Blair concludes the walk, leading the way to one of the many neighborhood brunch spots, you'll be humming along with Cab and craving some soul food.

BARBÈS • 124

BAR4 • 128

BROOKLYN ACADEMY OF MUSIC/
BAMCAFÉ • 129

BROOKLYN CONSERVATORY
OF MUSIC • 130

CELEBRATE BROOKLYN
FESTIVAL • 132

CENTER FOR
IMPROVISATIONAL MUSIC • 137

GALAPAGOS • 138

HANK'S SALOON • 139

ISSUE PROJECT ROOM • 140

THE MONTAUK CLUB • 142

NIGHT AND DAY • 143

PUPPETS JAZZ BAR • 145

SISTAS' PLACE • 146

ST. ANN'S WAREHOUSE • 149

TEA LOUNGE • 150

ZEBULON • 151

BROOKLYN & QUEENS

BARBÈS

376 9th Street at Sixth Avenue, Park Slope
☎ 718 965 9177 · www.barbesbrooklyn.com
🚇 Seventh Avenue F
🚇 Fourth Avenue F/N/R

EXPATRIATE FRENCHMAN OLIVIER CONAN AND VINCENT DOUGLAS HAPPENED ONTO THIS boarded-up former laundry site in summer 2001, in hopes of launching a neighborly performance space. As musicians with a half-dozen different bands between them, the pair had precise ideas about what to book and how to stage it. And they had a name for their enterprise: Barbès, taken from the funky neighborhood in Paris where the teenaged friends spent their days and evenings, awash in the North African culture that defined its street life. That they knew nothing about running a bar has proven, luckily, not to be an issue in the success of this charming street-corner spot.

If anything, these songsters-slash-entrepreneurs have created one of the city's best-loved hangouts. The shoebox-like space divides between a front bar and a back room, with a postage-stamp stage, an upright piano, and tables and chairs for about 30 people (60 in SRO mode). An illuminated "Hotel d'Orsay" sign dangles from the rear right corner wall, seemingly snatched right from the Rue de Lille. Though, as Conan points out, it actually was salvaged from the old Ansonia Clock Factory building on Seventh Avenue, and had seen time as a movie prop. (Even the name itself has resonance: Cinephiles will recall the hotel as the one occupied by Jean-Louis Trintignant in *The Conformist*.) The tin ceiling is a vibrant crimson, which puts the well-read jazz fan in the mind of what Paul Desmond once said about Ornette Coleman's music: "It's like living in a house where everything's painted red."

The music here takes on many more hues. Weekends are occupied by old-timey string bands and the Django Reinhardt specialist Stephane Wrembel, while the co-owners often showcase their polyglot ensembles, such as Las Rubias del Norte (Mexican ballads and boleros) and Chicha Libre (1970s Peruvian party music). Jazz, of all sorts, fills the rest of the calendar, which taps into the wealth of talent that resides in Park Slope and nearby neighborhoods. Now more than ever, in fact, as there has been a steady influx of musicians chased out of Manhattan by escalating rents. At the same time, downtown venues such as the Knitting Factory and Tonic, which had built reputations as hubs for forward-thinking jazzers, shifted focus. Barbès seized the moment. It's the epicenter of what might be called a new "downtown" scene.

"Musicians were living in Brooklyn but there wasn't a scene before," says Anthony Coleman, a pianist and composer who lives in the East Village but often finds himself riding the F train to Park Slope for gigs. "It's not like the scene is dead here, but Brooklyn is where it's gone. I never thought of Park Slope as a happening place, but Barbès gave it focus."

Local heroes such as Tony Malaby, Oscar Noriega, and Tim Berne have adopted the venue as a roost, with weekly slots held down by the boisterous Balkan brass band Slavic Soul Party and the recurring residency of violinist-about-town Jenny Scheinman. The venue is a sure bet for anyone looking to discover what's next on jazz's horizon. "It's really changed a lot in the last few years," says Michael Attias, the saxophonist who books the club's weekly Night of the Ravished Limbs series, devoted to new jazz. "There was a big void."

Musicians love the sound of the listening room, which possesses some acoustic mojo no one can pin down. "It's live, but not boomy," says Attias, who also dismisses the notion that "because we play 'weird' music, we deserve to play in the ugliest, shabbiest, stinkiest place." Barbès is the opposite of the noble dives that stirred the music's new waves in decades past. It's warm and inviting (and, as of late 2006, still serving $4 draft). "The truly subversive thing is to take this music and put it in this elegant, relaxed setting."

BRASS AND THE BALKANS

B Y DAY, MATT MORAN IS A MAD SCIENTIST OF THE VIBRAPHONE, ONE OF THE BUSIEST improvisers on the downtown New York scene. By night, he snatches up his tapan—a bass drum of Macedonian origin, made out of goatskin—to lead his comrades in Slavic Soul Party. The bust-loose party band is booked every Tuesday night "forever" at Barbès, where it blurts with enough brass and bang to make a marching band rumpus out of popular themes from the Balkan region, which loosely encompasses Bulgaria, the former Yugoslavia, and Albania. Unlike similar acts on the scene, the group's agenda is never strictly folkloric, nor is it a stab at injecting rock or electronic elements into traditional sounds—the mode of the more pop-oriented Balkan Beat Box, which features alto sax wiz Ori Kaplan. Though the music is fervently researched, it's filtered through the reeds of post-modern jazz players who bring their own swerve to the off-kilter rhythms and keening melodies—the stuff of weddings, funerals, and festival booze-ups. It's not such an unlikely premise.

"A big part of it is the rhythmic phrasing," Moran says, noting how the music's scales and melodies filtered down from Turkish sources. "There's a lot of 'snake-time' that's related to jazz and free improvisational phrasing. The challenge is how to make something sound mysterious and groovy at the same time." Though brass band music from around the world has begun to enjoy a vogue among listeners restless for an accessible exoticism, Balkan-themed acts have been part of the New York jazz scene since the early 1990s. Groups like Pachora, Paradox Trio, and Dave Douglas's Tiny Bell Trio applied folk melodies to improvisation, around the same time that the so-called Radical Jewish Culture movement reclaimed klezmer as a source material. Frank London, a member of the Klezmatics, was a key player in that scene, and also continues to explore various traditional sounds with his troupe, the

Klezmer Brass All-Stars—which jumbles Balkan and Middle European themes with the funk pulse of the Brazilian carnival.

Some musicians embraced this movement as a way to reconnect to their own heritage. But bands like Slavic Soul Party, whose members include Japanese and Latino musicians, are more simply compelled by a fervor for the music—and a love of the global brass band tradition. Sometimes, the band does it by indulging the familiar, sliding into the parallel universe of the New Orleans brass band, with bumptious tubas that would make perfect sense on a Missy Elliott remix. It's almost certain that the Balkanized version of the Mardi Gras classic "Ya Ya" is the only one credited to both Lee Dorsey (who scored the original 1950s hit) and Goran Bregovich. "You hear this music at first and you think, 'Damn, it's so funky, but what the hell is it?'" Moran says. "But what kept me in it is the depth and beauty and unalloyed intensity of it. It makes us want to play the most beautiful, powerful, groovy thing we can. We need chops of steel, if we're going to play for hours anyway."

BAR4

444 Seventh Avenue at 15th Street, Park Slope

☎ 718 832 9800 · www.myspace.com/bar4

🚇 15th Street F

THOUGH KNOWN MORE FOR DJS DROPPING LATE-NIGHT BEATS AND MONDAY NIGHT DRINK SPE-cials, this corner bar features live jazz a couple of nights a week. Sunday's "Konceptions" series is curated by pianist and composer James Carney, a one-time student of bass legend Charlie Haden who has shared the bandstand and studio with the likes of Ravi Coltrane, Christian McBride, and Nels Cline. The performances showcase new music by young players in an informal atmosphere that holds about 50-60 listeners.

BROOKLYN ACADEMY OF MUSIC/BAMcafé

30 Lafayette Avenue between Lafayette
& Ashland Streets, Fort Greene
☎ 718 636 4100 · www.bam.org
🚇 Atlantic Avenue 2/3/4/5/B/D/Q
Pacific Street M/N/R Fulton Street G
Lafayette Avenue C

THOUGH ITS NEXT WAVE FESTIVAL STICKS MOSTLY TO THE CONTEMPORARY CLASSICAL HIT PARADE (Kronos Quartet, Philip Glass, Bang on a Can), the Brooklyn Academy of Music also strives to be a cultural center reflective of the city's grassroots art scenes. Since 1997, BAMcafé—upstairs from the huge lobby of the Peter J. Sharp Building—has staged small-scale performances from every genre. Jazz is prominent, with an eye towards bold thinkers and innovative fusions of improvisation with Jewish, African, and Asian influences. Chances are, you may wander into the airy, sparkling 200-seat café (which serves a short-order menu of panini, satay, and burgers), and encounter something as fresh as the post-modern brass ensemble TILT or the free-style clarinet of 1960s vanguardist Perry Robinson. There also are frequent nods towards musicians from Fort Greene. The neighborhood has long been an artist's enclave, claiming Walt Whitman and Marianne Moore as residents, and emerged in the 1980s as a hothouse for African-American creatives (such as Spike Lee) and, more recently, a fast-gentrifying arts district, anchored by BAM and the Mark Morris Dance Center. BAMcafé's weekend evening shows overlap with the mainstage events, which creates an amiable, after-party vibe. No cover charge, but a drink and a snack quickly meets the $10 minimum.

BROOKLYN CONSERVATORY OF MUSIC

58 Seventh Avenue at Lincoln Place,
Park Slope
☎ 718 622 3300
www.brooklynconservatory.com
🚇 Grand Army Plaza 2/3
🚇 Seventh Avenue B/Q

GOOD SPOT TO CATCH PROMISING JAZZ CLASSICAL TALENTS IN RECITAL. AND TOO EASILY OVER-looked. The monthly jazz series presents a cross section of the music's more entertaining names, whether it's a vocalist with pop affinities like Vanessa Rubin, a bebop great like pianist Barry Harris, or a fiery salsa band. The walls of the 1881 Victorian Gothic brownstone are full of secrets: They first sheltered the Park Slope Masonic Club.

SONNY ROLLINS AND THE WILLIAMSBURG BRIDGE

JAZZ HISTORIANS LOVE TO DISAGREE, BUT YOU WON'T FIND MANY DISPUTING THAT 1959 WAS an abundant, pivotal year for the music. Miles Davis, Ornette Coleman, and Charles Mingus all recorded classic albums that signified not only artistic vitality, but a form in a heady, transitional stage. The 1960s had begun. But where was Sonny Rollins? The tenor saxophonist had dropped off the scene. Though some of his peers knew where to find him—John Coltrane would practice with him—Rollins had plunged head-long into "retirement." It was anything but, however, as one of jazz's most distinctive soloists was simply "woodshedding." Rollins chose a spot high on the Williamsburg Bridge, not far from his home, to sharpen his chops. He played day and night. Sooner or later, a fan with keen ears was bound to solve the mystery and, sure enough, a writer named Ralph Berton heard Rollins one night, "riding the pulse of a non-existent rhythm section." A subsequent issue of *Metronome* ran the exposé, though Berton kept the particulars vague—even changing Rollins' name. But the secret was out. As Rollins told writer Francis Davis, in the liner notes to a reissue of *The Bridge*—the album with which he ended his two-year sabbatical—he chose to retreat after a disappointing gig in Baltimore. "I felt like I wasn't delivering," he said. And began a course of dedicated self-improvement. Jazz lore doesn't get much more romantic. It's irresistible to think of Rollins as the role model for countless, nameless sax players blowing in the moonlight, with the Manhattan skyline in the backdrop. But the reality is: Only one of them will ever be Sonny.

CELEBRATE BROOKLYN FESTIVAL

Near the entrance at 9th Street
& Prospect Park West, Park Slope

☎ 718 855 7882 · www.celebratebrooklyn.org

🚇 Seventh Avenue F

EVERY SUMMER, THE CELEBRATE BROOKLYN FES-
TIVAL SERIES DRAWS 250,000 FANS TO PROSPECT
Park for mostly free performances by an eclectic range
of artists—mostly musicians, but also dancers and
others—as well as cult film screenings and thoughtful
original programs that are one-of-a-kind. Jazz bookings are scattered through the season, which runs
mid-June to mid-August and parallels Central Park's
splashier Summerstage series. Fans can expect to
catch big names (Wynton Marsalis, James Carter) and
slightly more esoteric entertainers. "Saturday Night
Live" musical director Hal Wilner has been known to
produce some of his crazy quilt tribute concerts here,
casting local jazz heroes like trumpet bad-ass Steven
Bernstein or guitarist James Blood Ulmer in all-star
salutes to Neil Young or Leonard Cohen, for instance.

The program began in 1979 as part of a broader
urban renewal initiative launched by the New York
City Department of Parks and the Brooklyn Borough
president. "The landscape was quite different then,"
recalls Jack Walsh, the festival's director. "The park
was in terrible shape." The 1939 bandshell, situated
then as now near the entrance at Prospect Park West
and Ninth Street, was derelict, blanketed in graffiti.
Residents feared traversing the grounds after dark. As
Walsh notes, the idea of staging concerts was "radical
at the time." But the concept was popular, and became
a way to present locally-based artists—particularly jazz
legends, such as Randy Weston or Max Roach, as well
as scrappy, up-and-coming dance troupes—as a way
to reclaim the park. The bandshell, renovated in 1982
and 1998, faces a natural amphitheater with a 7,000-

person capacity (seats for 2,000) and offers surprisingly crisp acoustics. The programs have grown increasingly broad, targeting various international communities within Park Slope and adjacent neighborhoods (with lots of African and Latin-themed evenings).

THE LOUIS ARMSTRONG HOUSE

34-56 107th Street, Corona

☎ 718 478 8274 · www.satchmo.net

🚇 103rd Street/Corona Plaza 7

THE LOUIS ARMSTRONG ARCHIVES

Queens College

65-30 Kissena Blvd., Flushing

☎ 718-997-3670 · www.satchmo.net

🚇 71st Avenue & Continental Avenue

Forest Hills V/R/E/F

Bus: Q 65 to Jewel Avenue and 150th Street

QUEENS'S MOST-CELEBRATED JAZZ RESIDENT IS QUITE A BIT MORE THAN A MEMORY. BESIDES conceiving the template for jazz trumpet, instigating the concept of solo improvisation, and becoming a pop vocal artist widely loved beyond the jazz realm, Louis Armstrong was a loyal neighborhood guy. He was deeply invested in the daily life around his modest brick home in Corona, where he moved in 1943. He also was pack rat, errr—relentless collector of his own ephemera, that is—and so, more than 30 years after his death in 1971, there exists an abundance of Armstrong effects and memorabilia. It's in the collection of the Louis Armstrong House & Archives at Queens College, to which a visit is more uniquely rewarding than many such places. Much of that has to do with Armstrong himself, a character of marvelous self-invention who could easily have sprung from the depths of American folklore if, in fact, he had not already risen from the hazard-strewn streets of New Orleans. Even the date given as his birthday—July 4, 1900—

has a mythic ring to it: born with the century, on Independence Day. Well, who else so fully exemplified jazz? The singularly American art form began as the creative expression of musicians only a generation removed from slavery. It doesn't really matter that Armstrong—who was also called Pops, or Dippermouth, or Satchelmouth or Satchmo—was actually born a little more than a year later. Like so much in his life, it just makes for a better story. That Armstrong preserved so much of that story while still alive and blowing strongly has guaranteed a healthy afterlife that isn't limited to his recorded musical legacy—or the many movie cameos he made during his glory days.

A $1.6 million restoration of the home he shared with his fourth wife, Lucille, was finished in October 2003, and the house, at 34-56 107th Street, is open to the public. It's a must-see, if not for Lucille's extravagant notions of interior design, then for Louis's hi-fi fetish, which caused him to put speakers in the ceilings and wire his office with more electronics than the Nixon White House.

The actual archives are housed in a library space at Queens College, which has been overseen by archivist Michael Cogswell since 1991. The collection includes more than 5,000 items. These number a remarkable trove of 650 reel-to-reel audio tapes made by Armstrong, recorded between the early 1950s and the week before his death. (The tapes are gradually being converted to CD format so visitors can listen to the recordings.) He also displays a visual flair, as each box of tape is decorated with an original collage, often made from cut-up newspaper and magazine clippings about Armstrong or his contemporaries. In one, an image of King Oliver—Armstrong's trumpet-playing forebear—hoists his horn from an imaginary stage inside a clipping of the artist's head.

It's those sorts of details you have to love. Poster-size blowups of Armstrong's letters are, as might be expected, laden with frisky humor. There are samples of risqué poetry; a holiday card with a photo of him sitting on a toilet (as viewed through a keyhole)—the musician was a great advocate of the laxative Swiss Kriss, and gave it away to friends and fans; and a Cannabis Cup awarded posthumously by *High Times* magazine (Armstrong was also a big fan of marijuana, and titled an unpublished volume of his autobiography "Gage," which was a slang term for the weed). The Archives curates accordingly, with an affectionate wink. One of its recent exhibits: "Love Me or Leave Me: Louis and His Four Wives."

CENTER FOR IMPROVISATIONAL MUSIC

295 Douglass Street between Third & Fourth Avenues, Carroll Gardens

☎ 212 631 5882 · www.schoolforimprov.org

🚇 Union Street R

TRUMPETER RALPH ALESSI RUNS THIS NIFTY VENUE, A NON-PROFIT MUSIC SCHOOL THAT offers a unique double-bill most Saturdays: a workshop from 4 p.m. to 6 p.m., followed by an 8 p.m. concert. The instructor/performers have included a who's who of the most inventive contemporary jazz bandleaders and instrumentalists: Jason Moran, Mark Helias, Fred Hersch, Bill Frisell, Henry Grimes, Jim Black, Don Byron, Nasheet Waits, Uri Caine, Mark Turner, and Ravi Coltrane, whose Yamaha grand piano occupies the concert space. Alessi, whose career includes stints with Steve Coleman's Five Elements, Tim Berne, Sam Rivers, and many of the artists who visit his school, launched the center in 2001, and has operated from its current location—a former soap factory in Carroll Gardens—since 2005.

"We don't have a lot of resources to advertise, so right now attendance is driven by who's playing," Alessi says. "Most people come from a circle of musicians who I'm involved with, so I know them all on some level." The space, which accommodates about 40 patrons, also serves as a classroom for intensive, week-long summer sessions. "I believe in the idea. The educational thing is, first and foremost, what we're trying to do."

GALAPAGOS

70 North 6th Street between Kent
& Wythe Avenues, Williamsburg
☎ 718 384 4586 · www.galapagosartspace.com
🚇 Bedford Avenue L

BURLESQUE SHOWS, UNDERGROUND CINEMA, POETRY SLAMS, ART EXHIBITS, LITERARY READINGS—it's all here at this bar and gallery housed in the site of a former mayonnaise factory. Named for the South Pacific archipelago that became the foundation of Charles Darwin's research, this venue certainly harbors a lot of fascinating flora and fauna. Galapagos is the best-known of numerous new creative venues that began springing up in Williamsburg in the 1990s. It's both a neighborhood hangout and curatorial realm, as likely to stage a reading by Zadie Smith as a bedazzling performance by the World Famous Pontani Sisters. Jazz sneaks in, usually in the guise of new-fangled string bands or a set from any number of younger musicians in the teeming neighborhood talent pool.

HANK'S SALOON

46 Third Avenue at Atlantic Avenue

☎ 718 625 8003 · www.exitfive.com/hankssaloon/

🚇 Atlantic Avenue 2/3/4/5/B/D/Q, Pacific Street N/R/M

ABOUT THE LAST PLACE ANYONE MIGHT MISTAKE FOR A JAZZ HANG, HANK'S SITS AT THE corner of an urban industrial strip—Brooklyn's Third Avenue—not far from the borough's downtown civic district. Looming plans for massive overhaul of the Atlantic Yards by uber-developer Bruce Ratner, complete with Frank Gehry skyscrapers and a basketball arena for the future New York Nets, casts a shadow over the entire area. It would be a shame to lose this ramshackle shrine to cheap drinks and good times. The building's mud-brown exterior is enlivened by telltale flames, crudely flaring in yellow and red paint, like the label on a bottle of hot sauce or the tattoo bulging on a burly biker's Popeye-sized forearm. What tornado swept through rural Alabama and snatched this roadhouse into the skies, only to deposit it within spitting distance of the Long Island Railroad?

Don't ask. Just enjoy. The pub and poolroom hosts a late-night jam session every Wednesday that belies its rowdy-on-down reputation.

ISSUE PROJECT ROOM

400 Carroll Street at Gowanus Canal
between Bond & Nevins Streets, Carroll Gardens
☎ 718 330 0313 · www.issueprojectroom.org
🚇 Carroll Street F/G

YES, IT'S A SILO.
NO, THIS IS NOT NEBRASKA.

The Issue Project Room is unique, even among the loft-and-warehouse art spaces that define the city's non-profit creative strata. When Suzanne Fiol, the resourceful director of the venue, lost her original spot in the East Village in 2005, she latched onto this uncommon site—a remnant from the days when the Gowanus Canal was a thrumming avenue for shipping. The two-story structure is fully rehabbed with ceilings as high as the proverbial elephant's eye, and rises up from grassy acreage adjacent to the ripely aromatic waterway.

The property has an uncanny feel, especially after dark. Lights from the towers of downtown Brooklyn flicker in the near distance, while the venue sits obscure behind massive iron gates. Though it's a mere two blocks from Smith Street—Brooklyn's bustling restaurant row—and equally close to a nascent nightlife district along once-industrial Third Avenue, the IPR seems to materialize out of nowhere.

Despite this (or perhaps because of it), the venue has attracted an impressive range of performers from all kinds of creative media. Experimental jazz, chamber music, and electronic excursions are dominant if not entirely definitive elements on the calendar, which might boast a theremin summit or a workshop reading with half the cast of *The Sopranos*. You might catch Joan La Barbara, the great soprano and exponent of John Cage's music, the writer Grace Paley sharing one of her short stories, or Steve Buscemi, the actor-director who is a notable booster of the venue. On occasion, organic-food theme dinners are organized around such concepts as the cinema of John Cassavettes. Fiol has forged ongoing partnerships with composer Pauline Oliveros and her Deep Listening Institute, and hosts residencies with outfits such as the Ne(x)tworks Ensemble.

Something about the space ties all these diverse activities together. "It's outrageous," says Fiol, "People tell me it's their favorite building in the whole city." Performances are staged in a circular upstairs room, which offers a lot of variety. An array of 16 speakers dangles from the ceiling, though more conventional stereo is also used. Beer, wine and, occasionally, snacks are available downstairs, except on nights when special meals are catered. The vibe is informal, and admissions generally under $15. The effect, most nights, is like a salon, with a passionate focus on the way various art forms can connect with each other. The open-minded atmosphere allows artists to flex their whammy without the concerns of playing more profit-driven rooms.

Fiol occupies the space in the shadow of massive real estate development throughout the once-disdained blocks around the canal. Yet, she is happy to be a nomad if that leads her to such interesting discoveries as the new IPR. "If I was going to have to go anywhere," says the photographer and former gallery director, "this is where I would want to go."

THE MONTAUK CLUB

25 Eighth Avenue at St. John's Place, Park Slope

☎ 718 638 0800 · www.montaukclub.com

🚇 Seventh Avenue B/ Q, Grand Army Plaza 2/3

JAZZ IS AN OCCASIONAL FEATURE AT THIS HIST-ORIC SITE, MEMORABLE AS A REGAL LOCATION in the independent film *Illuminati*, a period piece directed by John Turturro—who lives nearby. A vestige of Park Slope's emergence as an upper-crust bedroom community in the late 19th century, the still-active private organization opened the doors to its Venetian Gothic clubhouse in 1891, when the adjacent blocks were at the peak of a real estate boom. Famous guests included Teddy Roosevelt. The club remains right proud of its architectural and design features—the delicately hued stained glass, the rich mahogany. Glance at a membership roster from way back when and many familiar personages show up. These include the men who built Brooklyn as we knew it, such as railroad men Richard Schermerhorn and Charles Pratt, whose surnames now abide on street signs, sub-way stops, and colleges. There is surely no more opu-lent backdrop for a downbeat. Check the website for concert listings.

now called Biscuit

NIGHT AND DAY

230 Fifth Avenue at President Street, Park Slope
☎ 718 399 2161 · www.nightanddayrestaurant.com
🚇 Union Street R

COLE PORTER, COCKLES CON CHORIZO, AND MORE. FANS OF THE WEST VILLAGE STANDBY CORNELIA Street Café will find this restaurant and performance space a tad familiar. It's the same formula, nudged across the Brooklyn Bridge and into Park Slope. The dining and bar area occupies a sizable chunk of street corner, with al fresco seating and scarcely a vacant table on weekends. The eclectic menu underwrites the nightly performances staged in the gaily christened Starlight Room at the rear of the building.

Bookings juggle cabaret vocalizing—by first-rank stars such as Mary Cleere Haran—literary fare, and jazz residencies. Trumpeter John McNeil is one recent mainstay. Owner Robin Hirsch, who also runs Cornelia Street Café, hopes to continue drawing on long-term artistic friendships to create a buzz. His partner is Judy Joyce, whose family owned the defunct, and legendary, old school writer's hangout the Lion's Head Pub, in Greenwich Village. Where once sat a neglected Fifth Avenue noodle house, Hirsch sees a bohemian grove. "Park Slope is the epicenter of musicians and writers in America," Hirsch proudly proclaimed, having abandoned Manhattan to take up residence in an adjacent brownstone. "It's not improbable that some of the older Lion's Head characters who did not die of cirrhosis will read here," says Hirsch, alluding to a crew that once included writers such as Nat Hentoff, Pete Hamill, and Nick Tosches.

The Starlight Room, so-called for its glass ceiling, is compact and brightly lit, with a piano that sits before a fresco that depicts an art deco tableaux of Cotton Club-era New York. There are chairs and tables for about a dozen couples, more when weather allows outdoor seating. Cover charges are low, and there's a lot to choose from on the agreeably offbeat bar menu. Though seasoned jazz listeners may prefer the more intensive focus at its sister venue on Cornelia Street, Night and Day is a work-in-progress. Its programs likely will evolve as more dinner patrons discover what's going on down the hallway past the kitchen.

PUPPETS JAZZ BAR

294 Fifth Avenue at 2nd Street, Park Slope
☎ 718 499 2627 · www.puppetsjazz.com
🚇 Union Street R, Fourth Avenue F/R

THIS SPARTAN VENUE IS DEFINITELY ALL ABOUT THE MUSIC. THE NARROW SPACE HAS TABLES and chairs for about 20 guests and a small bar that serves beer and wine. Owner Jamie Affoumado named the club in honor of his days as a 1970s skateboarding legend, when he was part of the "Zoo York" crew. His friends called him "Puppethead" for the weightless way he seemed to hang in mid-air, neck aswivel, when he pulled a 360. The versatile soul, who still commutes from the Bronx, plays drums most nights, backing up a range of musicians that includes local resident Arturo O'Farrill (pianist son of fabled bandleader Chico) and well-traveled bassist Alex Blake. If location is key, Puppets has a lock: Foot traffic is heavy along this stretch of Fifth Avenue, which is thick with upscale restaurants like the Blue Ribbon Grill and Stone Park Café, and kooky little shops. The late-evening sets, which begin after 9:30, wisely aim to lure the after-dinner crowd.

SISTAS' PLACE

456 Nostrand Avenue off Jefferson Avenue,
Bedford-Stuyvesant

☎ 718 398 1766 · www.sistasplace.org

🚇 Bedford Avenue/Nostrand Avenue G

Nostrand Avenue A

THIS COMMUNITY CENTER AND COFFEEHOUSE HAS A MOTTO: "WHERE JAZZ—MUSIC OF THE spirit—Lives and Culture Is a Weapon." The space lives up to its social activist intentions, with political forums and poetry workshops. Bedford-Stuyvesant, the setting for Spike Lee's edgy comedy-drama *Do the Right Thing*, has seen a wave of gentrification in recent years and is sorting out its identity as a community. The late stateswoman and Presidential candidate Shirley Chisholm was born here, as was the hip-hop mogul Jay Z. Jazz events are always top-notch. Frequent guests include the violinist Billy Bang, former Sun Ra trumpeter Ahmed Abdullah, bassist William Parker, and drummer Lewis Nash—as well as vocalists and emerging talents. Check website for most current listings as jazz dates are irregular.

THE QUEENS JAZZ TRAIL TOUR

FLUSHING TOWN HALL

137-35 Northern Blvd., Flushing
☎ 718 463 7700 · www.flushingtownhall.org
🚇 Flushing-Main Street 7

THOUGH MANHATTAN HAD MOST OF THE NIGHT-
LIFE, THE SPRAWLING BOROUGH OF QUEENS
was—historically—where many of jazz's great names
actually went home to sleep. The fact is not lost on
the Flushing Council on Culture, and Flushing Town
Hall, which does its best to promote the local jazz
legacy through exhibits, concert performances, and
a popular Saturday morning bus and walking tour.
The Queens Jazz Trail Tour is a three-hour jaunt in
an old-fashioned trolley style bus through the jazzi-
est parts of Queens. Louis Armstrong's Corona is a
primary stop, including peeks inside Joe's Artistic
Barber Shop—where Satchmo had his hair cut—and
the house where Armstrong lived. Tour guide Coby
Knight— a cordial amateur vocalist and doo-wop war-
rior who grew up in Corona with fond memories of its
African-American musicians and sports champs— is
quick to remind everyone that it's not all about Louis.
Dizzy Gillespie also lived in the neighborhood, as do
Clark Terry and Jimmy Heath today. Other residents
of Queens, at large, included Charles Mingus, Roy
Eldridge, Buddy Rich, Lennie Tristano, Milt Jackson,
Benny Goodman, John Coltrane, Mal Waldron, Lester
Young, and Bix Beiderbecke.

A visit to the Armstrong archives at Queens
College (see page TK) sketches in much about the
trumpeter's home life, one frequently devoted to entertaining grinning posses of kids from the block. And
a further jog into St. Albans, and a walking tour of
Addisleigh Park, explores a neighborhood where the
top black entertainers of their day enjoyed a kind of

exclusive community. Count Basie, Ella Fitzgerald, Fats Waller, James Brown, and Lena Horne all called its verdant lawns home. The trend began in the 1920s, as segregation deterred the performers from buying homes elsewhere. Until his death, the bassist Milt Hinton would welcome tour groups into his house for a brief look-see and some refreshments. And even though Count Basie's Olympic-sized swimming pool is a thing of the past, his old spread now subdivided, there's still a chance to bump into a few characters.

ST. ANN'S WAREHOUSE

38 Water Street at Dock Street, DUMBO
☎ 718 254 8779 · www.artsatstanns.org
🚇 York Street F, High Street A/C

ENJOY IT NOW. SECOND ONLY TO THE BROOKLYN ACADEMY OF MUSIC AMONG THE BOROUGH'S major arts presenters, St. Ann's may not remain at its current home, a 14,000-square-foot former spice milling factory, after its current lease expires in 2007. The art space's impeccable track record has survived one major move already. Founded in 1980 and hosted at St. Ann's and the Holy Trinity Church in Brooklyn Heights, the non-profit Arts at St. Ann's kept its name after relocating to its new spot in 2001 following disputes with the church. Early on, its programs won a reputation for innovative musical tributes—the genre-blurring producer Hal Wilner enjoyed a virtual residency there—and for attracting the leading edge of songwriters, composers, and creators of mixed-media spectacles. Given room to roam at its new venue, Art's at St. Ann's is a bit of the 1980s SoHo/East Village performance scene transposed and souped-up. The likes of Laurie Anderson and the Wooster Group have staged productions there, but so too has cultural icon Al Pacino, avant-garde puppeteer Janie Geiser, and blues legend Othar Turner (with Wim Wenders running around the stage filming the show). Blue-chip jazzers such as guitarist Bill Frisell and trombone legend Roswell Rudd, among others, have found St. Ann's a welcome resource for developing and presenting new concepts. The space, which can hold 1,200, is almost too spacious, but the organization has done a good job of dressing up the cavernous sprawl so it doesn't feel like the backlot of a convention center. The abandoned warehouse across the street is the historic Empire Stores building, which is slated for redevelopment as part of the Brooklyn Bridge State Park project.

TEA LOUNGE

837 Union Street near Seventh Avenue, Park Slope
☎ 718 789 2762 · www.tealoungeny.com
🚇 Seventh Avenue B/Q, Union Street R

DEPENDING ON WHAT HOUR YOU VISIT, THIS CUSHIONY CAFFEINE OUTLET IS VARIOUSLY A study hall, a nursery, a self-help salon, and an uncommon late-night hang. Its Israeli owners tout some 60 varieties of tea—including such seeming (to the uninitiated) esoterica as tang ting kuka cha—plus coffee, in all their soy double latte grandeur, Belgian beers at its full bar, snacks, and healthy salads. The interior's Salvation Army décor and the surplus of politically aware flyers are reminders that the venue occupies a prime spot across the street from bohemian Brooklyn's holiest of holies: the Park Slope Food Coop, the nation's largest such enterprise. Can nirvana be far behind?

Indeed, it is not. Wednesdays through Fridays, stellar jazz (and jazz-ish) combos hasten the approaching Godhead. Part of an eclectic calendar, the musicians are top-notch—all regulars from the neighborhood circuit—or will be in a few years. The prevalent laptops are a turnoff, as is the sprawlingly casual layout, but the lounge is a handy option to feed spur-of-the-moment musical cravings. Perhaps one of those nursing tykes will become the next Charlie Parker.

ZEBULON

258 Wythe Avenue at North 3rd Street, Williamsburg
☎ 718 218 6934 · www.zebuloncafeconcert.com
🚇 Bedford Avenue L

A FRENCH TRIO (GUILLAUME BLESTEL AND JEF AND JOCELYN SOUBIRAN) WITH A BACK-ground in the Manhattan club scene have basically brought the cooler aspects of East Village bar life across the river. Zebulon could easily be a new Avenue C music spot. The layout is inviting (dark wood prevails) with a Continental vibe, a long bar on one side of the room, and staging area in the back. The beer and booze selections are sophisticated, the short order menu a welcome option for night owls, and the management as enthusiastic about their enterprise as they hope their patrons will be. No cover charge for nightly music performances, which lean toward music in African, Caribbean, and South American styles. There's rock-solid jazz at least once a week, as avant-garde veterans like Charles Gayle and Eddie Gale mix it up with rising pyros like the Gold Sparkle Trio. Star session drummer Kenny Wollesen holds down a regular spot on the calendar. The demure storefront entrance may be tricky to spot, so watch for the gleaming stainless steel diner Relish, which sits across the avenue in retro-1950s glory.

JAZZ FESTIVALS • 154

JAZZ RADIO • 158

INSTITUTIONAL JAZZ • 160

LOST JAZZ SHRINES • 162

FESTIVAL OF NEW TRUMPET
MUSIC • 164

THE MASKED ANNOUNCER'S
HIT PARADE • 166

BIG BANDS • 169

BEYOND THE CLUBS

JAZZ FESTIVALS

JVC JAZZ FESTIVAL

JVC Jazz Festival: Various sites each June.
www.festivalproductions.net

Jerry Stiller, playing George Costanza's holiday-crazed
father on "Seinfeld," had a word for it: Festivus.
Translation: The season when everyone celebrates
with huge meals and endless gatherings. Jazz fans
in New York have their own Festivus, which begins
in late May, sprawls across the entire month of June,
and spills over into July. Different years bring different sponsors, organizers, and themes, but the most
consistent—if not always the most creative—of the
summer's big events is the JVC Jazz Festival. Mas-
terminded by George Wein, the promoter behind
the fabled Newport Jazz and Folk Festivals of the
1950s and '60s, and the massive New Orleans Jazz &
Heritage Festival, the citywide June jazz summit has
been a staple of Manhattan life since 1972. Wein was
forced to move his event from the open-air setting of
Newport, R.I. (a smaller festival has since been reacti-
vated), after unruly crowds scared off the city fathers.
The inaugural season was auspicious. A July 4 concert paired the Charles Mingus orchestra and Ornette
Coleman—performing "Skies of America" with the
American Symphony Orchestra—on a double-bill at
Philharmonic Hall.

That was 34 years ago. As the roster of jazz giants
has dwindled, Wein's festival has struggled for rele-
vance. He's also traded fire with critics who were perhaps too eager to send the now-81-year-old entrepre-
neur out to pasture. Not so fast. Throughout the 1990s,
the Knitting Factory's upstart "What Is Jazz?" fest
grew bigger each year as sponsors (Heineken, Texaco,
Bell Atlantic) came and went. By 2000, it had become
the dominant New York jazz festival, splitting June
evenly with Wein (JVC runs for two weeks, beginning
in mid-June), and incorporating major mainstream
names into its mix of downtown favorites and rock

acts (such as Sonic Youth and Stereolab). Blink. Within a year, Wein's outfit—Festival Productions—snatched the financially shaky Knitting Factory's main sponsor, Verizon, and put on a second, smaller late-summer festival (since discontinued) that featured concerts identical to what the venue then typically programmed. Dominance ensured, Wein has subsequently become a touch more inventive with his primary summer smorgasbord. Recent fests, while still broadly tribute-oriented (Bix Lives!), continued a welcome expansion from major concert halls and parks into small clubs such as the Village Vanguard, and tapped into a new generation of players to complement the blue-chip bookings of Ornette Coleman, Wayne Shorter, Keith, Jarrett and other major artists who first made their names in the 1960s. "The jazz press has often seized upon emergent activity as an excuse to cast our festival in an adversarial role," the not-unprickly Wein writes in his memoir, *Myself Among Others: A Life in Music*. "…This epidemic started as far back as the late '50s." Unfazed, the promoter sticks to his program, and still finds time to jump onstage and play a little piano.

VISION FESTIVAL
Various locations TBA
www.visionfestival.org

Miraculously, the Vision Festival—an artist-run event with roots in the Lower East Side jazz collectives of the 1980s—arrives each June to present a giddy abundance of music and dance performances produced on budgets tighter than a bulldog's leash. The event, which has grown in prominence and influence during its first decade, runs for about a week parallel to the JVC, though such matters are always subject to change. Each year's performance site is similarly unpredictable. But artistic director Patricia Nicholson Parker has displayed an uncanny knack for securing offbeat, and often historically significant, venues to host the shebang. During its 11-year run, the non-profit festival has been housed in a dilapidated former synagogue, the basement of a Greek Orthodox church, a rehab center that had once been the site of 1960s rock palace the Electric Circus, and the Knitting Factory, whose own corporate-backed (and since defunct) summer festival it ostensibly rivaled once upon a time. Now, through sheer persistence, the festival has become an institution of its own, though its rejection of corporate sponsorship keeps the focus purely on the music. And everything else but the kitchen sink, as concerts mingle generations of forward-minded musicians, dancers, poets, and visual artists in marathon evenings that unwind as leisurely as a potluck supper. Between sets, get to the concession stand and you can enjoy festival co-founder William Parker's fried chicken, while taking in an exhibit of vintage jazz photography or conversing about the latest new releases with visitors from Portugal or Finland. Though firmly devoted to honoring an avant-garde lineage that stretches back to the 1960s, the festival is full of surprises. Sympathetic artists from the indie-rock and electronic worlds—such as Cat Power, Yo La Tengo, and DJ Spooky—have headlined, while elder statesmen like Sam Rivers and Fred Anderson have enjoyed generous tributes. Rumors float about a possible move above Fourteenth Street this year, which would put the festival in more direct competition with JVC and in shouting distance of Jazz at Lincoln Center, the very sort of establishment to which it offers a minority report about what matters in jazz history.

CENTRAL BROOKLYN JAZZ FESTIVAL

http://centralbrooklynjazz.blogspot.com

This annual festival convenes each April to celebrate the legacy of Brooklyn's jazz scene of the 1950s and 1960s, with concerts scheduled at various spots in Fort Greene, Clinton Hill, and Bedford-Stuyvesant. Headliners have included Eddie Gale, James Spaulding, Odean Pope, Andrew Cyrille, Robert Glasper, and Randy Weston.

RIVER TO RIVER FESTIVAL

Free concerts summer-long in Battery Park City
and other downtown sites
www.rivertorivernyc.com

An eclectic and seemingly endless series of free concerts and related events at various public spaces in TriBeCa, ranging from the South Street Seaport area to a stretch of parks adjacent to the Hudson River. Jazz is a featured component, as is the Bang on a Can marathon. The 10-1/2 hour festival, which focuses on contemporary classical music with rock, electronic, jazz, and world-music elements prominent, opened its 2006 spectacle with a composition for 100 tubas. It was composer Anthony Braxton's 61st birthday, and though the piece was subdued rather than chaotic, the notion was remarkable enough to make someone hope the organizers will try to top it in 2007.

THE JAZZ IN JULY FESTIVAL

1395 Lexington Ave. at East 92nd Street
☎ 212 415 5500 · www.92Y.org

The impeccable Bill Charlap has taken over the bench from Dick Hyman, the pianist and historian who built this series into a New York favorite. The annual celebration of vintage jazz is staged at the 92nd Street Y.

LINCOLN CENTER OUT OF DOORS

Various sites at Lincoln Center
throughout August
www.lincolncenter.org

Huge, free, al fresco concerts staged across the multiple plazas and green spaces of the Lincoln Center campus. Programs touch on everything from Brazilian dance festivals to Louisiana zydeco, and few summers slip by without a sprawling performance by Sonny Rollins.

JAZZ RADIO

WHEN IT COMES TO JAZZ BROADCASTING IN NEW YORK, BIRD IS THE WORD. EVERY WEEKday morning, longtime radio host Phil Schaap plays the music of Charlie Parker on WKCR-FM (89.9), the non-commercial station based at Columbia University. Schaap, affectionately known as the "Bird Nerd," hits the air at 8:20 a.m., and keeps it filled with sometimes rare recordings and lots of savvy aficionado banter. It's the stuff of classic radio—evoking not only the bop of yesteryear, but the era when radio was still the dominant form of electronic media and New York was in post-war creative ferment.

WKCR's signal first crackled about the time Parker and his cohorts were revolutionizing jazz: 1941. Initiated as a student radio club with transmissions limited to dorm rooms, the station went public on October 10. The first record to spin was "Swing Is Here," featuring Gene Krupa and Roy Eldridge. Jack Kerouac, then a Columbia student, would have had his ear glued to the dial. And, as Schaap notes in an extensive interview on the station's website (www.wkcr. org), Bela Bartok—who taught music at Columbia—was an occasional guest, petitioned for his thoughts on Coleman Hawkins's "Body and Soul."

Six decades on, WKCR continues to program copious (but not exclusively so) amounts of jazz, with 30-year veteran Schaap and his fellow hosts on hand to ensure an in-depth historical focus that is also obsessively anecdotal. The station is famous for its marathon celebrations of a particular artist—playing nothing but Thelonious Monk or Eric Dolphy on their birthday, or perhaps the anniversary of their death—which can stretch to as long as 12 days. During one such festival, in July 1979, honoree Miles Davis phoned up WKCR a lot. During one such conversation, which lasted two hours, Schaap recalls jotting down a long list of Japanese-only Davis discographic information as the temperamental trumpeter dictated. "He said, 'You got it?'

I said, 'Yes, Mr. Davis.'—I Mr. Davis-ed him the whole week, to be truthful. And he said, 'Good. Now forget it. Forget it. And play *Sketches of Spain* right now!' So I walked into master control, and just to make it more dramatic, I picked up the needle with the pot [volume knob] up, and plunked it down hot."

Some other jazz radio options:

WBGO-FM (88.3): Newark-based public radio station programs jazz 24/7. Along with shows overseen by longtime hosts such as Michael Bourne ("Singers Unlimited," Sundays at 10 a.m.) and Walter Wade ("Fillet of Soul," Sundays at 6:30 p.m.), the station carries the full range of NPR syndicated jazz programs. [www.wbgo.org]

WNYC-FM (93.9): Cultural institution Jonathan Schwartz spins American popular song, including the great jazz vocalists, Saturdays and Sundays at noon. Also: "Big Band Sounds" with Danny Stiles, the "Vicar of Vintage," 8 p.m. Saturdays on the station's other outlet, AM 820. [www.wnyu.org]

WFMU-FM (91.1): As its motto states, this Jersey City-based community radio station has been "freeing your ass so your mind can follow since 1958." Jazz occasionally intrudes on the madly eclectic shows—which go by names like "Inflatable Squirrel Carcass"—programmed by a diverse and quirky array of volunteer DJs. Bethany Ryker's Sunday night "Stochastic Hit Parade" (10 p.m.-midnight) is often a treat, with live interviews and performances from downtown faves, and no lack of conceptual bravado ("Brass Meets Bollywood" is a typical theme). [www.wfmu.org]

INSTITUTIONAL JAZZ

MANY MUSEUMS, UNIVERSITIES, AND NON-PROFIT ARTS ORGANIZATIONS PRESENT JAZZ throughout the year, or on specific occasions. Here's a shortlist of institutions that offer interesting and consistent programming.

THE NEW SCHOOL

55 West 13th Street, 5th floor
between Fifth & Sixth Avenues
☎ 212 229 5896 x305 · www.newschool.edu/jazz
🚇 14th Street F/L/V/1/2/3

The jazz program at the downtown university, located near New York University and the West Village, has quite a reputation in town. Its faculty includes such players as Cecil Bridgewater, Jane Ira Bloom, Andrew Cyrille, Joe Chambers, Chico Hamilton, Junior Mance, Benny Powell, Reggie Workman, and many others. And its roster of graduates boasts some of the most promising younger jazz musicians in the field: Brad Mehldau, Chris Potter, Roy Hargrove, Peter Bernstein, Miri Ben-Ari, Susie Ibarra, Jesse Davis, and Walter Blanding Jr. Live performance is a constant here, from faculty concerts to special collaborative events featuring guest artist-educators in league with their students, as well as solo and ensemble recitals. Times vary, but there's frequently something going on in the Jazz Performance Space, a fifth floor venue where admission is always free and open to the public.

LAGUARDIA PERFORMING ARTS CENTER

47th Avenue at Van Dam Street
Long Island City, Queens
☎ 718 482 5151 · www.lagcc.cuny.edu/lpac
🚇 33rd Street 7

The venue at LaGuardia Community College in Queens

features jazz in its mix, presenting a variety of programs, including celebrations of Queens's jazz heritage, Latin-themed concerts and evenings focused around specific musicians.

ROSE CENTER FOR EARTH AND SPACE

at the American Museum of Natural History
81st Street at Central Park West
☎ 212 769 5200 · www.amnh.org
🚇 81st Street B/C

Live jazz, under the Sphere at what is also known as the Hayden Planetarium, is presented the first Friday of each month, with sets at 5:45 and 7:15 p.m. Free with regular museum admission. Bookings have included well-regarded jazz veterans, such as Jimmy Heath, Lou Donaldson and David "Fathead" Newman.

SYMPHONY SPACE

2537 Broadway at West 95th Street
☎ 212 864 5400 · www.symphonyspace.org
🚇 96th Street 1/2/3

Imaginative jazz programs are a highly visible component of this uptown non-profit venue's extensive calendar of performances, readings, and screenings. Home to the World Music Institute, as well as two separate theaters (including the Leonard Nimoy Thalia, named after its "Star Trek" star patron), Symphony Space is best known to jazz fans for its annual "Wall-to-Wall" concerts. The free, day-long events unite a seemingly irrational array of artists around the music of a single composer. Miles Davis and Joni Mitchell have been previous subjects, while the names on the musicians' call sheet would reflect smartly in anyone's record collection. There are evenings built around individual leaders (such as Don Byron, Jason Moran) and their concepts, and quasi-jazz occasions that are compelling for their trans-genre overlap.

LOST JAZZ SHRINES

TRIBECA PERFORMING ARTS CENTER

Borough of Manhattan Community College

199 Chambers Street, #S1105C,

at West Side Highway

☎ 212 220 1460 · www.tribecapac.org

🚇 Chambers Street 1/2/3

ANYONE WHO SAT THROUGH EVEN AN HOUR OR TWO OF KEN BURNS'S EPIC DOCUMENTARY *Jazz* knows that the music could never have moved forward without all the feverish activity in its engine rooms: the clubs. Whether it was Minton's Playhouse in Harlem, where bebop was incubated in the early 1940s, or the Village Vanguard, where John Coltrane and many others recorded historic live sessions in the 1950s and '60s, the intimacy and intensity of these spaces gave jazz room to breathe and grow.

Though Burns' knack for sepia-toned montage coated so much of this history in the shellac of nostalgia, it's important to know that the vital spark that animates jazz is very much here and now. The ongoing Lost Jazz Shrines series succeeds brilliantly at reconciling those two poles of jazz experience. Produced by the Tribeca Performing Arts Center, part of the Borough of Manhattan Community College, the eight-year-old program each year focuses on a celebrated jazz club that no longer exists—yet played a critical role in the development of the music—evoking an era through panel discussions, performances, and exhibits.

One recent season was devoted to Café Society, the Sheridan Square club where Billie Holiday famously debuted the song "Strange Fruit" in 1939 for an integrated audience. Owner Barney Josephson, a shoe salesman from New Jersey whose parents immigrated from Latvia, opened the L-shaped basement club a year earlier as a place where blacks and whites, fans and entertainers, could mingle on and offstage. Clare Booth Luce came up with the name, and, as befits the then-editor of *Vogue*, it spoofed the pretensions of the uptown crowd.

"The club's motto was 'The wrong place for the right people,'" says Willard Jenkins, a Washington, D.C.-based jazz writer and producer who curates the series. "We were interested in it because of its strong sociological aspects. Barney Josephson was someone who loved jazz, who loved black music, but when he went up to the Cotton Club, he didn't like what he saw there. He saw black performers onstage, but not in the [all-white] audience. He opened the first fully-integrated club."

Don't expect note-for-note evocations of time, place, and persona, however. The concerts reflect more on an artist's inspiration than some *American Idol*-style emulation. "The music is based very loosely on what they did," says Carla Cook, who has performed in the series. "I can't tell you the impact Ella Fitzgerald made on me," says the Fort Greene resident, who saw the singer with guitarist Joe Pass when she was still a teenager living in Detroit. "It was one of those moments you don't forget. You can't really have a foundation in this music without these masters."

The Lost Jazz Shrines series was initiated in 1998 by 651 Arts in Brooklyn, which spearheaded productions in eight cities nationwide, and collaborated with TPAC and Aaron Davis Hall in Harlem on New York programs. It was a one-time deal. But TPAC, which first had presented concerts and panels focused on the 1970s "loft jazz" scene, decided to carry on, adopting the concept as ideal for its mission. Subsequent series have looked at the clubs the Five Spot, the Half Note, and Slug's, all of which are commemorated in a photo exhibit adjacent to the theater.

"Personally, I'm a jazz enthusiast," says Linda Herring, the center's executive director, "and I felt like, instead of doing contemporary music, we should program something that has a stronger resonance but isn't done a lot. Also, jazz clubs are not as much fun as they used to be. They give you 45 minutes and you're out of there."

FESTIVAL OF NEW TRUMPET MUSIC

Dates and locations vary.
Current information at www.fontmusic.org

IF SOMEONE ONLY THOUGHT OF THE TRUMPET IN TERMS OF DIXIELAND PARADES OR MILES Davis slinking in his iconic silhouette of the early 1960s, they'd be in for a lot of surprises at the Festival of New Trumpet Music. The upstart event, which originated in 2003, celebrates the most fundamental of jazz instruments as pivotal to the music's contemporary evolution. FONT Music, as it's called, is a month-long series of concerts curated by leading trumpeters Dave Douglas and Roy Campbell Jr., along with Jon Nelson, from the avant-garde chamber group Meridian Arts Ensemble. Exact dates and venues change each year, but the festival typically occurs after the regular summer jazz season, at a variety of mostly downtown venues.

Louis Armstrong invented jazz as we know it when he first uncorked improvisations in a group context in the mid-1920s. Thirty years later, Davis reclaimed the horn as a symbol of his own detached and mercurial intellect. Since the 1980s, Wynton Marsalis has been the world's best-known trumpeter, thanks partly to his institutional platform at Jazz at Lincoln Center. But FONT rejects such tidy summaries. Rather than dwell on the history of the instrument, it offers perspectives on its future. Though many of the artists on the roster may be familiar to New York jazz fans, more than half of the fest's 40-plus performances are slotted for emerging players. Styles are all over the map. Much is recognizably jazz, both arranged and improvised, acoustic and electronic. But there are intriguing deviations, whether gypsy brass bands from Eastern Europe, an all-trumpet orchestra, or thoughtful tributes to departed masters like Lester Bowie.

"I got sick of hearing that there's only two kinds

of trumpet players," says Douglas, a prolific composer and bandleader who often sees his name juxtaposed with that of Marsalis, as if they were the flip sides of a coin. "You know, outside and inside," he added, using jazz lingo for musicians who slip free of standard form, or remain steadfast about familiar musical structure. "Each trumpeter we present is a completely unique world unto themselves. This is the time to expose how broad this music is, and break down some of the boxes people put it into."

Though it does a good job of showing off some of the leading talents who work just outside the jazz mainstream, the festival is not particularly bound to even the avant-garde canon. "We want to blur all the lines," says Nelson, whose ensemble commissions new pieces for its chamber concerts, and has adapted the music of Frank Zappa for brass. "It's easy for people to put things in a box, and when events like this are institutional, it's the death of something that could have had some interesting possibilities."

THE MASKED ANNOUNCER'S HIT PARADE

JOEL DORN WAS ONLY 25 WHEN HE SCORED HIS DREAM JOB: PRODUCING MUSIC FOR ATLANTIC Records. The Philadelphia native, a disc jockey and mysterious television pitchman known as "The Masked Announcer," was lucky to work during the label's classic era, 1967-1974, and won most attention for a pair of Roberta Flack hits, "The First Time Ever I Saw His Face" and "Killing Me Softly," for which he nabbed Grammy Awards. Dorn also befriended, championed, and produced some real jazz legends—most notably and notoriously Rahsaan Roland Kirk, the blind multi-reedist known for playing three horns simultaneously.

Dorn, now producing reissues of jazz, R&B and gospel sessions for Hyena Records (www.hyenarecords. com), recalls some of his favorite jazz performers and sessions. When you hear his voice, gruff, warm and resonant, it sounds like a late-night FM radio DJs from the 1960s, which is exactly what Dorn was.

RAHSAAN ROLAND KIRK: When we did that first record for Atlantic, *The Inflated Tear*, it went on to become a minor classic. We did that in Webster Hall—one of those gigantic studios where they could record the Philadelphia Orchestra or a Broadway score, that was Columbia's big studio. It was a church, I think, originally, and then it became a studio. This gigantic room. We darkened the whole room except for a little spotlight. Rahsaan and his guys were in the middle of this room. It was the size of a hockey rink that place. And they made all the music in this little spotlight, and they were in a gigantic room which was pitch black except for the light that fell on them. And there was a vibe on that music, it was like guys on a streetcorner in an abandoned city. And it had a very street feel to it, itinerant musicians stopping to play someplace. It was an oil painting in my brain. As he and I recorded, it got crazier and crazier. *Blacknuss* and *Volunteered Slavery* and *The Three-Sided Dream*, it was like a lunatic asylum.

YUSEF LATEEF: The same way I recorded Rahsaan, I remember recording Yusef Lateef. I always was interested in people who were one of a kind and had world-class chops and that's kind of all that rings my bell. Kirk was double one-of-a-kind. Same with Yusef. As explosive as Kirk was, Yusef was very controlled, very literal, very everything—he poured his heart into the music. I would come up with the concepts. If he bought into the concepts, he'd come back with the music. I'd give him a concept like "Yusef Lateef's Detroit" or "The Blue Yusef Lateef." He would come back with just the most interesting collection of things. And you couldn't scare him with an idea. I was heavy into Magritte—REALLY heavy into Magritte—and Fellini, when I was making those records, and if I would come in with some abstract, surreal concept, it didn't shake Yusef. He'd let me do stuff NOBODY would let me do.

LES McCANN: Les, his records never really matched what he did in the clubs. I found out what it was that bugged him. He didn't like the idea of "Take one, take two." You'd run out of tape just when he was getting warmed up. So we hooked up two machines and just went back and forth from one to the other so he never had to stop. That little thing. I never said "Take one." So we got that first record. We had a half-hit on it. Then we hooked him up with Eddie [Harris], and it really took off.

JIMMY SCOTT: That first Jimmy Scott session was unbelievable. It was called *The Source*. To me, it has nothing to do with me. That's the Jimmy Scott that you never heard. You put that with the Ray Charles record on Tangerine, *Falling in Love Was Wonderful*, you'll understand, the people who got Jimmy Scott, what it was that they got. He was unbelievable, in those years, when he had his fastball.

MAX ROACH: I did some stuff with Max Roach with choirs. There were two albums. One was called *Members Don't Get Weary* and the other was called *Lift Ev'ry Voice and Sing*. They were really vital. There was a tension in the room. Max had these choirs. He was reinterpreting spirituals but with an explosive black consciousness driving the train. There were like incredible moments. Those two records were really great social commentaries. They were so well conceived that you can't help but get a message, the message that he wanted to deliver. He had young guys with him full of fuckin' butane. Billy Harper, George Cables, those cats. When you listen to them, it might not be like pleasant listening. But you'll understand where people were. It captures a certain energy that existed at that time and does not exist now. But when it was existing, a lot of people took shots at it and Max really nailed it.

Those sessions were both at Atlantic. That's where I preferred to record. Eleven West 60th. That was the end of the classic era. When they moved to 75 Rock it became something else. You go into that studio and you could have anyone from Aretha to Bette to Cream to the Rascals to the Drifters. You should only know what those walls heard. So when they busted that out, man, a lot of us were just pissed. You know what's there now? There's a wig shop. And probably a travel agent's. The corner—where Nesui's office was, where Ahmet's office was—is a wig shop, and they have like 30 or 40 heads in the window. When you walk by there, it's like, how the fuck did this happen? You know, you're a kid. You think it's gonna last forever.

BIG BANDS

MONDAY NIGHTS IN NEW YORK BELONG TO BIG BANDS, AND SEEMINGLY ALWAYS HAVE. THE institution began February 8, 1966, when an 18-piece ensemble led by composer-arrangers Thad Jones and Mel Lewis opened what was to be a three-week run of Monday evening performances at the Village Vanguard. Trumpeter Jones, the brother of drummer Elvin and pianist Hank, was a veteran of Count Basie's band, and drummer Lewis had toured with the orchestras of Stan Kenton and Gerry Mulligan. The outfit was called The Jazz Band, though it would soon bear its leaders' names: The Thad Jones/Mel Lewis Orchestra. The original lineup featured Bob Brookmeyer, Hank Jones, Richard Davis, and Snooky Young, among others, and won immediate notice from John Wilson in *The New York Times* as it "ripped through Thad Jones's provocative, down-to-earth arrangements with the surging joy that one remembers in the early Basie band or Woody Herman's first Herd."

Forty years later, the band—now billed as the Vanguard Orchestra—still plays every Monday. But... why? "Back in the '70s, there was a lot of work for jazz musicians in studios and on Broadway, but the theaters were dark on Mondays," explains Steven Bernstein, a trumpeter and composer who leads his own Millennial Territory Orchestra, a pop-friendly outfit that crosswires Basie with Prince in its erstwhile residencies at venues like Tonic and the Jazz Standard. "So Monday night was when you put together your big bands. It was the only night you could get enough musicians together."

Unlike the glory days of swing, when the bands stomped hard and played for dancers, the ensembles that work the New York club scene are mostly just for listening. There are the so-called "ghost" bands, like the Duke Ellington Orchestra, and bands led by active composer-arrangers like Maria Schneider. There are repertory outfits that are extensions of arts institutions, like the Lincoln Center Jazz Orchestra, and off-the-wall concepts like the Bjorkestra, a group that features jazzy arrangements of songs by the Icelandic pop singer Björk.

Sadly, the tradition is slowly dying. The nature of "big band" music has moved off the road, where young players learned firsthand by sharing the bandstand with more seasoned performers, into the college classroom, where it becomes an academic exercise.

One strong exception to that trend is the Mingus Big Band, which currently presides over Tuesday nights at Iridium. The group originated in 1991, when the management of the now-defunct club Fez invited Sue Mingus (the bassist's fourth wife, widow, and posthumous torchbearer) to debut a Mingus ensemble, hoping to add some substance to its bookings. As Sue Mingus remembers, the big band took a slot on the calendar "between a nipple piercing demonstration and an amateur night." The 12-14-piece group, whose members are drawn from a rotating pool of some 200 musicians, has become its own tradition. Its triumph is threefold: zesty musicianship; a reassertion of big band vibrancy that has long been in decline in the city's jazz clubs; and the remarkable animation of the Mingus canon, which knits together gospel, Afro-Caribbean, rhythm-and-blues, free jazz, and chamber music—usually with the stitches showing.

"He said, 'I'm trying to write the truth of what I am, and the reason it's different is I'm changing all the time,'" says Sue Mingus, an elegant yet formidable presence who maintains a humorously testy relationship with the musicians. Of course, while Mingus infamously punched in the teeth of his gifted trombonist Jimmy Knepper, the slim and patrician Mrs. Mingus is a good deal more genteel. She simply teases the musician who plays a solo too long or too loud when he comes by for his check. "In the old days, whoever was the leader of the band resented me," she says. "'Who is this woman screeching in the wings?' But then someone said, 'Who pays your checks? She's the leader.' It was a revelation. Now I take it and run with it." The weekly sets rarely skip the Mingus essentials: rousing, gospel-fired numbers like "Better Git Hit in Yo' Soul," and the roaring "Haitian Fight Song" (familiar from Volkswagen and Toyota commercials). But they also explore unknown territory, as Mingus composed much faster than he could get many of his pieces performed. While these Tuesday night summits showcase hot soloists taking a break from their own repertoire, they also are popular with performers—such as Elvis Costello—who like to drop in spontaneously. Which, naturally, is how Mingus would have liked it. He was, Sue Mingus writes in her memoir *Tonight at Noon*, "the ornery, sometimes violent, often unjust, blustery figure who fired his musicians onstage, hired them back, denounced the audience for inattention, picked fights, mastered his instrument, dominated his music, vented his political beliefs onstage, presented a larger-than-life personality, and created on-the-spot performances for all to see."

INDEX

52nd Street · 86
55 Bar · 20
5C Café and Cultural Center · 42
Allen, Woody · 95
Armstrong, Louis · 134
Arthur's Tavern · 22
Arturo's · 23
Barbès · 124
BAR 4 · 128
Big Bands · 169
Birdland · 74
Blue Note · 25
Bowery Poetry Club · 46
Brass and the Balkans · 126
Brooklyn Academy of Music/BAMcafé · 129
Brooklyn Conservatory of Music · 130
Café Carlyle · 95
Café St. Bart's · 76
Celebrate Brooklyn Festival · 132
Center for Improvisational Music · 137
Central Brooklyn Jazz Festival · 156
Chez Suzette · 77
Cleopatra's needle · 100
Coleman, Ornette · 64
Copeland's · 119
Cotton Club · 119
Cornelia Street Café · 27
Cutting Room, The · 68
David Gage Strings · 16
Detour · 45
Downtown Music Gallery · 52
Enzo's Jazz at the Jolly Hotel Madison Towers · 80
Fat Cat · 29
Festival of New Trumpet Music · 164
Five Spot Café · 64
Flushing Town Hall · 147
Galapagos · 138
Garage Restaurant & Café, The · 30
Gathering of the Tribes, A · 46
Gospel Brunches · 119
Hank's Saloon · 139
Harlem, Historic · 111
Harlem Jazz Strolls · 120
Iridium · 81
Issue Project Room · 140
JVC Jazz Festival · 154
Jazz Festivals · 154
Jazz at Lincoln Center · 82
Jazz Radio · 158
Jazz at St. Peter's Church · 91
Jazz Gallery · 12

Jazz in July Festival, The · 157
Jazz Museum in Harlem · 116
Jazz Record Center · 69
Jazz Standard · 88
Jimmy's No. 43 · 48
Joe's Pub · 50
Kitano, The · 92
Kitchen, The · 70
Knickerbocker, The · 51
LaGuardia Performing Arts Center · 160
Lenox Lounge · 108
Lincoln Center Out of Doors · 157
Louis · 54
Londel's Supper Club · 119
Louis Armstrong Archives, The · 134
Louis Armstrong House, The · 134
Makor · 101
Masked Announcer's Hit Parade, The · 166
Minton's Playhouse · 114
Mo Pitkin's House of Satisfaction · 55
Montauk Club, The · 142
New School, The · 160
Night and Day · 143
Nublu · 56
Paul, Les · 78
Puppets Jazz Bar · 145
Queens Jazz Trail Tour, The · 147
River to River Festival · 157
Rollins, Sonny and the Williamsburg Bridge · 131
Rose Center for Earth and Space at the American Museum
        of Natural History · 161
Roulette · 14
Rue B · 57
S.O.B.'s · 15
Showman's Café · 117
Sistas' Place · 146
Smalls · 31
Smoke · 102
St. Ann's Warehouse · 149
St. Nick's Pub · 118
Stone, The · 60
Sweet Rhythm · 34
Swing 46 · 93
Symphony Space · 161
Tea Lounge · 150
Tonic · 62
Triad Theatre · 104
Tribeca Performing Arts Center · 162
Village Vanguard · 35
Vision Festival · 155
WBGO-FM · 159
WFMU-FM · 159
WKCR · 158
WNYC-FM · 159
Zankel Hall · 94
Zebulon · 151
Zinc · 38

VALERIE TRUCCHIA

ABOUT THE AUTHOR

Steve Dollar writes about pop culture for a variety of publications, including *Newsday*, the *New York Sun*, *Time Out Chicago*, *Stereophile*, and *Print*. His articles also have appeared in *GQ*, the *Wall Street Journal*, and the *Oxford American*. He writes about jazz and other enthusiasms online at www.skronkboy.com. He lives in New York City.